HENRY FIELDING

The Author's Farce
(Original Version)

Edited by
CHARLES B. WOODS

LONDON
EDWARD ARNOLD (PUBLISHERS) LTD.

Printed in Great Britain by
William Clowes and Sons, Limited, London and Beccles

REGENTS RESTORATION DRAMA SERIES

General Editor: John Loftis

THE AUTHOR'S FARCE

At the time of his death on February 21, 1965, Professor Woods had been some years dedicated to editing the plays for the forthcoming Wesleyan University Press edition of Fielding's works. He had agreed to draw on this material at a later date to provide three plays for the Regents Series. His death left all this incomplete, and his work for the Wesleyan edition will have to be carried through by others. *The Author's Farce* was essentially completed, needing mainly mechanical adjustments to reduce its elaborate apparatus to the requirements of the Regents Series. This he had hoped to do during 1965. The Wesleyan Press has kindly allowed me to use the material so that the work, substantially as he would have prepared it, may appear in advance of their edition. I have modernized the text, stripped away much of the technical apparatus, and have redistributed the material in the introduction, notes, and appendices. Several paragraphs of the Introduction are adapted from a lecture, "Fielding as Playwright," that Professor Woods delivered to the Humanities Society of the University of Iowa in 1961. Occasionally I have had to supply material, but I do not think I have exceeded the proper role of a literary executor. Professor Edgar V. Roberts, who was to have provided the musical annotation for the Wesleyan edition and who will now complete the first volume of plays, has generously offered the tunes printed in Appendix C; Professor Eugene Helm has assisted me greatly in preparing these for publication.

CURT A. ZIMANSKY

University of Iowa

Regents Restoration Drama Series

The Regents Restoration Drama Series, similar in objectives and format to the Regents Renaissance Drama Series, will provide soundly edited texts, in modern spelling, of the more significant English plays of the late seventeenth and early eighteenth centuries. The word "Restoration" is here used ambiguously and must be explained. If to the historian it refers to the period between 1660 and 1685 (or 1688), it has long been used by the student of drama in default of a more precise word to refer to plays belonging to the dramatic tradition established in the 1660's, weakening after 1700, and displaced in the 1730's. It is in this extended sense—imprecise though justified by academic custom—that the word is used in this series, which will include plays first produced between 1660 and 1737. Although these limiting dates are determined by political events, the return of Charles II (and the removal of prohibitions against the operation of theaters) and the passage of Walpole's Stage Licensing Act, they enclose a period of dramatic history having a coherence of its own in the establishment, development, and disintegration of a tradition.

Each text in the series is based on a fresh collation of the seventeenth- and eighteeth-century editions that might be presumed to have authority. The textual notes, which appear above the rule at the bottom of each page, record all substantive departures from the edition used as the copy-text. Variant substantive readings among contemporary editions are listed there as well. Editions later than the eighteenth century are referred to in the textual notes only when an emendation originating in some one of them is received into the text. Variants of accidentals (spelling, punctuation, capitalization) are not recorded in the notes. Contracted forms of characters' names are silently expanded in speech prefixes and stage directions, and, in the case of speech prefixes, are regularized. Additions to the stage directions of the copy-text are enclosed in brackets. Stage directions such as "within" or "aside" are enclosed in parentheses when they occur in the copy-text.

Spelling has been modernized along consciously conservative lines, but within the limits of a modernized text the linguistic quality of the original has been carefully preserved. Punctuation has been brought into accord with modern practices. The objective has been to achieve a balance between the generally light pointing of the old editions, and a system of punctuation which, without overloading the text with exclamation marks, semicolons, and dashes, will make the often loosely flowing verse and prose of the original syntactically intelligible to the modern reader. Dashes are regularly used only to indicate interrupted speeches, or shifts of address within a single speech.

Explanatory notes, chiefly concerned with glossing obsolete words and phrases, are printed below the textual notes at the bottom of each page. References to stage directions in the notes follow the admirable system of the Revels editions, whereby stage directions are keyed, decimally, to the line of the text before or after which they occur. Thus, a note on 0.2 has reference to the second line of the stage direction at the beginning of the scene in question. A note on 115.1 has reference to the first line of the stage direction following line 115 of the text of the relevant scene. Speech prefixes, and any stage directions attached to them, are keyed to the first line of accompanying dialogue.

JOHN LOFTIS

Stanford University

Contents

Abbreviations

C.G.	Covent Garden Theatre
D.L.	Drury Lane Theatre
G.F.	Goodman's Fields Theatre
H.	The Little Theatre in the Haymarket
L.I.F.	Lincoln's Inn Fields Theatre
O1	Octavo, 1730
O2	another Octavo, 1730
O3	"The Second Edition," 1730
O4	"The Third Edition . . . Revis'd, and greatly Alter'd," 1750
S.D.	stage direction
S.P.	speech prefix

Introduction

The first edition of *The Author's Farce* was published "at Five o'Clock in the Afternoon" on March 31, 1730, the day following the first performance. A second printing, hard to distinguish from the first, followed, probably within a month.[1] A third, identified as "The Second Edition," came in July. From one of these a Dublin edition was printed in the same year. These rapid reprintings indicate the success of Fielding's play in its first version, but the extensive revisions for its revival in 1734 caused no such demand and this new version ("The Third Edition ... Revised, and greatly Alter'd") did not appear until 1750. Copy for this was a marked-up copy of the last of the 1730 London editions; while Fielding was undoubtedly responsible for the alterations in the text, he seems to have had nothing to do with the printing. This revised text was used by Murphy for the collected edition of 1762, the ultimate source of the later collected editions. Most readers know only this version of the play.

The following, then, are the significant texts:

O1   Printed for J. Roberts, 1730
O2   Printed for J. Roberts, 1730
O3   The Second Edition, printed for J. Watts, 1730
—   Dublin, printed by S. Powell, 1730
O4   The Third Edition, printed for J. Watts, 1750

Of these the Dublin edition is without authority (though it supplies the tune for Air II, unnamed in London editions) and its readings have not been recorded here; none would affect the text. O4 is such a thorough revision that recording all its variants would not be desirable, since it is in effect a new play. The radically different scenes are given in Appendix A; occasionally, where it is close to O1, attention is called to its readings in the explanatory notes.

[1] These first two octavos have not previously been distinguished. One is a page-for-page, though not always line-for-line, reprint of the other. The one presumably first, here designated O1, has leaf D3 unsigned and on p. 26 twice prints *Honeywood* for *Moneywood* in the scene heading. In O2 the press figure 6 appears on B8^v; on p. 39, l. 2, the word "at" is repeated.

The present edition is the first reprinting of Fielding's original version since 1730. The text rests on O1, collated with O2 and O3. Each of these has its own misprints and eccentric accidentals, but there are no substantive variants among the texts. Three speech prefixes at the beginnings of songs have been supplied; one (II.viii) has been changed; Fielding's variations in speech prefixes for his protagonist have been normalized.[2] There are no other departures from O1 except the modernization of the text.

The plays of Henry Fielding have rarely received high praise, despite the fact that some of them were extremely popular on the eighteenth-century stage. Nearly everyone who has commented on them during the last two centuries has felt obliged to concern himself with a question that may be put in this way: why should a comic writer of Fielding's ability have had such an undistinguished career as a dramatist? The most notable exception to this generalization is George Bernard Shaw, who expressed no doubt about the distinction of his career. In Shaw's opinion Fielding was the greatest practising dramatist, with the single exception of Shakespeare, produced by England between the Middle Ages and the nineteenth century. Without attempting to defend this estimate, which even to me seems somewhat rash, I hope the play here presented will show something of the quality of an experimental dramatist who worked during an unusually interesting period of English theatrical history.

It is perhaps not widely recognized that Fielding's dramatic activity coincided almost exactly with something of an explosion in the theatrical life of London. There were surprising increases in the number of playhouses and in the size of the theater-going public during the period 1729–1737. In the seasons immediately preceding the Licensing Act, Londoners often had their choice of four or five and sometimes even six performances on the same day, a situation without parallel since the early seventeenth century. Although Fielding and Lillo were the only active playwrights of the period who

---

[2] Luckless's speeches in Act III, where he is Master of the Show, are given as *Mast.* until the Bantomite interruption; his speech at l. 762 is headed *Luck. or Mast.*, then *Luck.* to the end of the play; in the Epilogue his speeches are headed *Auth.* (O4, like the present text, conveniently keeps "Luckless" through Act III but retains "Author" in the Epilogue.) There is one inconsistency in speech prefixes (carried over into O4 also): when the Bookseller enters at III.181 his speeches are headed *Book.*, but from l. 370 on, *Curry*; it has been normalized to the former.

are now remembered, it was truly a time of innovation and experiment when the theater was a lively and unpredictable institution—obviously much too lively for the government and the managers of the patent houses. The enormous success of *The Beggar's Opera* in 1728 had set the pattern for a new kind of irregular drama, the ballad opera (which usually had satiric overtones); when this genre was added to other irregular forms such as the short farce and the pantomime, which had already entrenched themselves in the repertory, popular interest in the conventional five-act forms of tragedy and comedy decreased to such an extent that on most evenings the theatrical managers found it prudent to add at least one irregular afterpiece to the stock five-act plays. Frequently the whole bill consisted of irregular productions.

Fielding's first play, in the conventional five-act form, *Love in Several Masques*, was produced in 1728, shortly before his twenty-first birthday. Presumably the young man had not yet decided upon a career in the theater, for within a month he had enrolled at the University of Leyden, where he remained as a student for almost a year and a half. During this period he sketched out the dialogue for some other dramatic works, and in 1729, when the news arrived that he could expect no more money from his father, the stage seemed to offer the most promising way to earn a living by his pen. The first four theatrical seasons that followed were the busiest in his life, with some fourteen plays produced. Irregular plays soon attracted him, and they were for the most part presented in the smaller playhouses, which were more hospitable to beginning playwrights than the patent houses. *The Author's Farce* was his first success in the new form, ushering in the period of theatrical vitality that was to be suffocated by the Licensing Act of 1737.

Presumably *The Author's Farce; and the Pleasures of the Town* was written during the winter of 1729–1730, not long before its production at the Haymarket on March 30. After Fielding returned from Leyden in the summer or autumn of 1729, he tried to get a play accepted by the patent houses but succeeded only in placing *The Temple Beau* at Goodman's Fields. His decision to ridicule the managers and the theatrical fare they offered must have been made after he became convinced that he would have to depend on the little playhouses for a livelihood, at least for a season or two. As a dramatist desperately in need of selling his wares, he soon saw that there was a market for "irregular" satiric plays with songs set to popular airs. In December

John Rich produced a fairly successful work of this type at Lincoln's Inn Fields, Forrest's *Momus Turn'd Fabulist*. In the early spring three similar plays, each satirizing popular entertainments, appeared almost simultaneously: Drury Lane brought out *Bayes's Opera* by Gabriel Odingsells on the same night *The Author's Farce* was first performed, and two nights later James Ralph's *The Fashionable Lady; or, Harlequin's Opera* had its first production at Goodman's Fields. One wonders whether this timing was deliberate and whose throat was intended to be cut. Odingsells said that his play had been written more than a year before its production; probably very little time elapsed between the completion of Fielding's script and the beginning of rehearsals.

The chief "literary" debts of *The Author's Farce* would appear to be to Farquhar for the frame play, and to Lucian, Buckingham, Gay, and Pope for the puppet show. Hints may have been picked up from Aristophanes, Jonson, Dryden, Congreve, Regnard, and many others. As might be expected in a piece of dramatic journalism, Fielding often echoes what newspapers, pamphlets, and satiric poems had been saying for years: it was really no news that the theaters were puppet shows, that pantomime and Italian opera were disgraceful entertainments for an intelligent people, that Orator Henley was a mountebank, that Cibber was an ignorant stage tyrant, and so on. It is the laughable way in which Fielding dramatizes such clichés that distinguishes *The Author's Farce* from the awkward and sometimes confused performances of writers like Odingsells and Ralph, who use similar material.

Four years after the great success of the first version, Fielding revised *The Author's Farce* to fit a quite different theatrical situation. He was now writing not for an irregular playhouse but for Drury Lane, under a management different from that he had attacked in 1730. Wilks and Booth were dead and Cibber had sold his share in the Drury Lane patent. At the opening of the 1733–1734 season a bitter feud had developed between the new patentees (John Highmore, Wilks' widow, and others), with whom Fielding sympathized as people whose legitimate investments were being jeopardized, and a rebel company of Drury Lane actors playing at the Haymarket under the direction of Theophilus Cibber.[3] Since the younger Cibber had fomented the rebellion, it is not surprising that the most striking

[3] A full account of this theatrical war is given in Arthur H. Scouten, *The London Stage*, Part III (Carbondale, Ill., 1961), pp. lxxxix–xciii.

addition to the reworked play is the figure of Marplay, Junior, one of Fielding's happiest satiric creations. The elder Cibber's elevation to the Laureateship, the rivalry between two opera companies, and the recently discovered corruption in the Charitable Corporation offered further themes. On the whole, the revision is almost conscientiously thorough, scarcely a page being left untouched. Political and social satire is sharpened,[4] and religious satire toned down. But the new material fails to mesh perfectly with the old; while the revision shows Fielding's increasing skill in some excellent passages it is less coherent and perhaps not quite so light-hearted as the original work, which had established his reputation as a comic playwright. It was coolly received when produced at Drury Lane in 1734 and was not printed until 1750, after the success of *Tom Jones*.

It would be difficult to exaggerate the importance of *The Author's Farce* in Fielding's dramatic career; its position is somewhat analogous to that of *Shamela* and *Joseph Andrews* with respect to his development as a writer of prose fiction. In these works his impulse to attack inspired him to experiment with satiric forms in which his talents for ridicule and criticism would find free expression. The wild burlesque of improbable denouements that rounds off *The Author's Farce* led directly to the parody of inflated tragedy in *Tom Thumb*. The puppet show staged by Luckless was a first study in techniques employed for the later dramatic satires such as *Pasquin* and *The Historical Register*. Finally, as the first ballad opera produced by Fielding, *The Pleasures of the Town* prepared the way for his most successful afterpieces, not to mention his longer efforts in the form. In a word, *The Author's Farce* is Fielding's pioneer work as a writer of irregular drama.

And it is in this kind of irregular drama that Fielding's excellence as a playwright lies. It would be difficult to exclude five of these plays from any selection of Fielding's best: *The Author's Farce*, *The Tragedy of Tragedies*, *Don Quixote in England*, *Pasquin*, and *The Historical Register*. It was unfortunate for the playwright's reputation that only *The Tragedy of Tragedies* could maintain itself on the licensed stage.

[4] Sheridan Baker, "Political Allusion in Fielding's *The Author's Farce, Mock Doctor*, and *Tumble-Down Dick*," *PMLA*, LXXVII (1962), 221–231, argues that "the first version [of *The Author's Farce*] is hardly less political than the second." But there seems to be little political satire in the 1730 text, and if Professor Baker's line of reasoning were followed, every stage production of the Walpole era that presented Punch and Joan or Harlequin would be politically suspect. However, there is nothing far-fetched about his seeing political implications in passages Fielding added in 1734.

The Licensing Act, to be sure, was not altogether responsible for the exclusion of the other plays; most of them depended so heavily on local hits and allusions for their best comic effects that audiences soon became incapable of identifying the specific targets, and a just appreciation of their ingenuity and satiric range is hardly to be acquired without a thorough exploration of the social, political, and theatrical background.

These plays desert the realistic approach of most Restoration and eighteenth-century comedy for the "Emblematical"—to borrow a term from the critic Sneerwell in *Pasquin*. The emblematical method as employed by Fielding is likely to give characters and plot an allegorical significance and often does not pretend to represent surface appearances of life as we know it. At times, however, what may be called non-realistic elements are juxtaposed or mingled with realistic elements in such a way that a peculiar satiric effect is gained, as in the hilarious ending of *The Author's Farce* when the symbolic or allegorical figures and the flesh-and-blood characters are shown to have family ties. Non-representational dramatic satire might have been Fielding's most valuable gift to the theater of his time, but unfortunately its promise as a liberator from outworn dramatic modes was never realized during the eighteenth century.

The Author's Farce was the first of Fielding's plays to be produced at the Little Theatre in the Haymarket. His *The Temple Beau* had been produced at Goodman's Fields, but the company in that theater, in its first year, was ill equipped for "irregular" entertainments; further, it may have been committed already to Ralph's *The Fashionable Lady* and in no position to handle another difficult production. In any event, the Haymarket in the west of London could expect to attract more fashionable audiences who would appreciate allusions that might fall on deaf ears in the City.

The *Daily Post* on March 18, 1730, announced as in rehearsal "a new Comi-Farcical Opera, call'd The Pleasures of the Town: being a Satirical Representation of all our late noted Publick Performances." The first performance took place on Easter Monday, March 30. The cast is listed in the published play. If none of the actors in this young company was to rise above the second rank, some of them seem to have acquired considerable skill in farce and burlesque. Jones, the speaker of the prologue, was apparently effective as Bookweight and Dr. Orator, since he went on to create more roles in Fielding's plays than any other actor. William Mullart, who had the role of Luckless, and his wife Elizabeth, who doubled as Mrs. Moneywood and the Goddess of Nonsense, formed a team which proved very useful to Fielding before they enlisted with Rich at Covent Garden for the season of 1734–1735. Michael Stoppelaer (Stopler), who played Sparkish and Signior Opera, was a young Irish tenor to whom Fielding assigned the romantic leads in three of his Drury Lane ballad operas; Stoppelaer later became a singer for Handel. James Lacy, who had the role of Witmore, never achieved great distinction as an actor, but as co-patentee of Drury Lane and Garrick's partner he has a place in the history of eighteenth-century entertainment.

The Author's Farce was Fielding's first triumph in the theater. It had forty-one performances at the Haymarket during the spring and summer of 1730; the third act had one additional performance when it was appended (somewhat incongruously) to *Hurlothrumbo* as *The Pleasures of the Town* on April 20. By April 18 Fielding's *Tom Thumb* was joined to it as afterpiece. On June 23, *Rape upon Rape*, Fielding's new five-act comedy, interrupted the run, of which there was only one more production, on July 3, to end the most successful opening season any play had enjoyed since that of *The Beggar's Opera* in 1728. Some of the notices indicate the extraordinary popularity of the play. After the first night the *Daily Post* announced: "None to be admitted into the Boxes but by printed Tickets, which will be delivered at . . . 5s. each. Pit 3s. Gall. 2s. where Places may be taken. N. B. There being a great Variety of Characters, to prevent any Confusion in the Action, no Person whatsoever can possibly be admitted behind the Scenes." The Prince of Wales attended on April 25 and May 14. Several times notices stated: "The Boxes not being equal to the great Demand for Places, at the particular Desire of several Persons of Quality, Pit and Boxes will be put together, and none to be admitted into either, and by printed Tickets, which will be delivered at the Theatre at 5s. each. Gallery 1s. 6d."

The first season over, the Haymarket players presented on Saturday, August 1, and throughout the following week a program at Reynolds' Great Theatrical Booth in Tottenham Court, in which the afterpiece was "A celebrated Operatical Puppet Show, call'd PUNCH's ORATORY: OR, The Pleasures of the Town. Containing several diverting Passages; particularly, a very elegant and learned Dispute between Punch and another great Orator. Punch's Family-Lecture: Or, Joan's Chimes on her tongue to some Tune. No Wires, all alive."

The Author's Farce opened the next season at the Haymarket on October 21, 1730, "With a new Prologue addressed to the Merchants 'Prentices of Great Britain." Miss Talbot replaced Miss Palms as Harriot, and there were a few other changes in the cast. *Tom Thumb* was added as afterpiece when the performance was repeated on October 23, but the popularity of *The Author's Farce* was waning. There were two further performances in 1730, each with changes of cast; for the latter of these Mrs. Nokes gave up her part of Mrs. Novel to take that of Signior Opera. There were at least twelve further performances before the Haymarket was closed for political reasons in June, 1731, but one of these seems to have been only of *Pleasures of the Town* and another without *Pleasures of the Town*.

The last performance of *The Author's Farce* at the Haymarket occurred on May 12, 1732; no other London performance of the entire play by living actors is known. Theophilus Cibber reduced it to a two-act afterpiece, in which he played Luckless, at Covent Garden on March 28, 1748.[5] Because Murdertext is listed among the characters, it is clear that Cibber worked with the 1730 text; indeed the revised version was not yet in print. Not unexpectedly, he deleted all material reflecting on his father: neither Marplay nor Sir Farcical appears in the elaborate playbill.

Scattered records of performances outside of London fail to reveal a single production of the play in its entirety. The York company gave *The Pleasures of the Town* in Newcastle in 1749, and the same afterpiece appeared fifteen times on the Norwich circuit during the period 1750–1758. Tate Wilkinson used the piece for his benefit in Dublin in 1763, and again in Edinburgh in 1764. The last known performance was at Bath, April 4, 1774.[6]

[5] This unexpected revival by Theophilus Cibber of a piece so hostile to the Cibbers has only now been explained. It was directly related to the curious puppet show staged by "Madame de la Nash" in Panton Street, Haymarket, from March 28 to June 2, 1748. That Madame de la Nash was merely the name under which Fielding operated was an ill-kept secret, and Cibber responded to Fielding's puppet-show Punch by reviving Fielding's flesh-and-blood Punch on the same night. See Martin C. Battestin, "Fielding and 'Master Punch' in Panton Street," *Philological Quarterly*, XLV (Jan., 1966).

[6] Performances by puppets were probably more numerous than the records indicate; see George Speaight, *The History of the English Puppet Theatre* (London, 1955), pp. 157, 331. There were performances by Richard Yeates in 1734 and 1735, and a notice in the *Daily Advertiser* for August 22 and 25, 1735, gives some information about them: "At the noted Yeates,

The stage history of the revised version is soon told. There were six performances, and six only, at Drury Lane from January 15 to January 21, 1734. For four of these six performances *The Intriguing Chambermaid*, also first presented then, was afterpiece, and it (acted by the same actors) became a permanent feature in the repertory. Obviously the cast was able enough. Many were from the original Haymarket cast—Mr. and Mrs. Mullart (Luckless and Mrs. Money-wood) and Jones (Bookweight and Dr. Orator) were in their old parts; Stoppelaer was again Signior Opera, but this time doubled as Marplay, Sr., since his old part of Sparkish had been deleted; Hicks, the original Joan, became Punch, and Hallam, who had created Dash, was given Punch. The most notable of the newcomers were Mrs. Clive (as Harriot and Mrs. Novel) and Charles Macklin (as Marplay, Jr.). If any comedians could have made the revival a resounding success, one supposes they would have done so in such suitable parts.

CHARLES B. WOODS

University of Iowa

Warner and Hind's Booth in London-Spaw-Fields, During the Time of the Welsh-Fair, will be perform'd the celebrated Opera call'd The Author's Farce: or, the Pleasures of the Town. With the comical Humours of Punch turn'd Orator, by their large Wax-Work Figures, being five Foot high, and have all the human Gestures of Life."

Bibliography

BAKER, SHERIDAN. "Political Allusion in Fielding's *Author's Farce, Mock Doctor,* and *Tumble-Down Dick,*" *PMLA,* LXXVII (1962), 221–231.

BANERJI, H. K. *Henry Fielding, Playwright, Journalist, and Master of the Art of Fiction.* Oxford, 1930.

BATESON, F. W. *English Comic Drama, 1700–1750.* Oxford, 1929.

CLINTON-BADDELEY, V. C. *The Burlesque Tradition in the English Theatre after 1660.* London, 1952.

CROSS, WILBUR L. *The History of Henry Fielding.* 3 vols. New Haven, 1918.

DUDDEN, F. HOMES. *Henry Fielding, His Life, Work, and Times.* 2 vols. Oxford, 1952.

FIELDING, HENRY. *Complete Works,* ed. William E. Henley. 16 vols. New York, 1903.

GAGEY, EDMUND M. *Ballad Opera.* New York, 1937.

HUGHES, LEO. *A Century of English Farce.* Princeton, 1956.

LOFTIS, JOHN. *The Politics of Drama in Augustan England.* Oxford, 1963.

NICOLL, ALLARDYCE. *A History of English Drama 1660–1900.* Vol. II, *The Early Eighteenth Century Drama.* Third edition, Cambridge, 1961.

ROBERTS, EDGAR V. "Eighteenth-Century Ballad Opera: The Contribution of Henry Fielding," *Drama Survey,* I (1961), 77–85.

SCOUTEN, ARTHUR H. *The London Stage,* Part III. 2 vols. Carbondale, Ill., 1961.

SHERBURN, GEORGE. "The Dunciad, Book IV," *University of Texas Studies in English,* XXIV (1944), 174–190.

SMITH, DANE FARNSWORTH. *Plays about the Theatre in England from The Rehearsal in 1671 to the Licensing Act in 1737.* London, 1936.

SPEAIGHT, GEORGE. *The History of the English Puppet Theatre.* London, 1955.

(Works relating to individuals represented in *The Author's Farce* are given in Appendix B.)

THE AUTHOR'S FARCE

Quis iniquiae
Tam patiens urbis, tam ferreus, ut teneat se?

Quis . . . se?] Juvenal I, 30–31: "Who can be so tolerant of this city, who so iron of soul, as to contain himself." The unquoted part of the first of these lines is one of Index's Latin mottoes in II.iv.

PROLOGUE

Spoken by Mr. Jones

Too long the tragic muse hath awed the stage
And frightened wives and children with her rage.
Too long Drawcansir roars, Parthenope weeps,
While every lady cries, and critic sleeps.
With ghosts, rapes, murders, tender hearts they wound,   5
Or else, like thunder, terrify with sound.
When the skilled actress to her weeping eyes
With artful sigh the handkerchief applies,
How grieved each sympathizing nymph appears,
And box and gallery both melt in tears.   10
Or when in armor of Corinthian brass
Heroic actor stares you in the face,
And cries aloud, with emphasis that's fit, on
Liberty, freedom, liberty and Briton.
While frowning, gaping for applause he stands,   15
What generous Briton can refuse his hands?
Like the tame animals designed for show,
You have your cues to clap, as they to bow.
Taught to commend, your judgments have no share;
By chance you guess aright, by chance you err.   20

But handkerchiefs and Britain laid aside,
Tonight we mean to laugh and not to chide.

In days of yore, when fools were held in fashion,
Though now, alas, all banished from the nation,
A merry jester had reformed his lord,   25
Who would have scorned the sterner Stoic's word.

---

3. *Drawcansir; Parthenope*] Characters in *The Rehearsal* (1671), the burlesque of heroic drama by Buckingham and others.
    11-16.] Appeals to patriotism and liberty in drama are frequent. Two recent examples were Benjamin Martin's *Timoleon* (D.L., Jan. 26, 1730) and James Thomson's *Sophonisba* (D.L., Feb. 28, 1730), both of which Fielding was soon to parody in *Tom Thumb*.

Bred in Democritus his laughing schools,
Our author flies sad Heraclitus' rules.
No tears, no terror plead in his behalf;
The aim of farce is but to make you laugh.   30
Beneath the tragic or the comic name,
Farces and puppet shows ne'er miss of fame.
Since then in borrowed dress they've pleased the town,
Condemn them not, appearing in their own.

Smiles we expect from the good-natured few;⎫   35
As ye are done by, ye malicious, do;   ⎬
And kindly laugh at him who laughs at you. ⎭

PERSONS IN THE FARCE

Men

LUCKLESS, the Author, and Master of the Show	*Mr. Mullart*
WITMORE, his friend	*Mr. Lacy*
MARPLAY ⎫ comedians	*Mr. Reynolds*
SPARKISH ⎭	*Mr. Stopler*
BOOKWEIGHT, a bookseller	*Mr. Jones*
SCARECROW ⎫	*Mr. Marshall*
DASH ⎪ scribblers	*Mr. Hallam*
QUIBBLE ⎪	*Mr. Dove*
BLOTPAGE ⎭	*Mr. Wells, Jr.*
JACK, servant to LUCKLESS	*Mr. Achurch*
JACK PUDDING	*Mr. Reynolds*
BANTOMITE	*Mr. Marshall*

Women

MRS. MONEYWOOD, the Author's landlady	*Mrs. Mullart*
HARRIOT, her daughter	*Miss Palms*

Persons in the Puppet Show

PLAYER	*Mr. Dove*
CONSTABLE	*Mr. Wells*
MURDERTEXT, a Presbyterian parson	*Mr. Hallam*
GODDESS OF NONSENSE	*Mrs. Mullart*
CHARON	*Mr. Ayres*
CURRY, a Bookseller	*Mr. Dove*
A POET	*Mr. W. Hallam*
SIGNIOR OPERA	*Mr. Stopler*
DON TRAGEDIO	*Mr. Marshall*
SIR FARCICAL COMIC	*Mr. Davenport*
DR. ORATOR	*Mr. Jones*
MONSIEUR PANTOMIME	*Mr. Knott*
MRS. NOVEL	*Mrs. Martin*
ROBGRAVE, the Sexton	*Mr. Harris*
SAILOR	*Mr. Achurch*
SOMEBODY	*Mr. Harris, Jr.*
NOBODY	*Mr. Wells, Jr.*
PUNCH	*Mr. Reynolds*

JOAN   *Mr. Hicks*
LADY KINGCALL   *Miss Clarke*
MRS. CHEAT'EM   *Mrs. Wind*
MRS. GLASSRING   *Mrs. Blunt*

The Author's Farce
and the
Pleasures of the Town

As acted at the Theatre in the Haymarket
Written by Scriblerus Secundus

ACT I

[I.i]   *Luckless's Room in Mrs. Moneywood's House.*
     Mrs. Moneywood, Harriot, *and* Luckless.

MONEYWOOD.

Never tell me, Mr. Luckless, of your play, and your play. I
say, I must be paid. I would no more depend on a benefit
night of an unacted play than I would on a benefit ticket in

Scriblerus Secundus] Martinus Scriblerus was the fictitious author created
by Swift, Pope, Gay, Arbuthnot, and other members of the Scriblerus Club
in 1713–1714, for whom they planned a whole series of pedantic works.
Three Hours after Marriage (D.L., 1717) by Pope, Gay, and Arbuthnot was
clearly in the Scriblerian spirit, as were to a lesser extent Gay's *Beggar's
Opera* (L.I.F., 1728) and Swift's *Gulliver's Travels*, 1726. In none of these
was the Scriblerus name used, but it was widely known in literary London
before it was affixed to *Peri Bathous, or, The Art of Sinking in Poetry* (1728),
primarily by Pope, and the prolegomena and notes to his *Dunciad Variorum*
(1729). Fielding's pseudonym shows him placing himself quite properly in
this satirical tradition; he used it for all his Haymarket plays of 1730 and
1731 with the single exception of the five-act *Rape upon Rape*, abandoning it
when he moved to Drury Lane in 1732.
[I.i]
    The opening scenes have enough of a resemblance to Act III of Farquhar's
Love and a Bottle for Fielding to be almost immediately charged with
plagiarism in *Candidates for the Bays, a Poem, Written by Scriblerus Tertius*
(London, 1730), pp. 9–10.

–7–

an undrawn lottery. Could I have guessed that I had a poet
in my house? Could I have looked for a poet under laced   5
clothes?

LUCKLESS.

Why not, since you may often find poverty under them?

MONEYWOOD.

Do you make a jest of my misfortune, sir?

LUCKLESS.

Rather, my misfortune. I am sure I have a better title to
poverty than you. You wallow in wealth, and I know not   10
where to dine.

MONEYWOOD.

Never fear that; you'll never want a dinner till you have
dined at all the eating houses round. No one shuts their
doors against you the first time, and I think you are so kind
never to trouble them a second.   15

LUCKLESS.

No, and if you will give me leave to walk out of your doors,
the de'el take me if ever I come into them again.

MONEYWOOD.

Whenever you please, sir, leaving you movables behind.

LUCKLESS.

All but my books, dear madam; they will be of no service to
you.   20

MONEYWOOD.

When they are sold, sir, and that's more than your other
effects would; for I believe you may carry away everything
else in your pockets, if you have any.

HARRIOT.

Nay, mamma, it is barbarous to insult him.

MONEYWOOD.

No doubt you'll take his part. Pray, get about your business.   25
I suppose he intends to pay me by ruining you. Get you in.
And if ever I see you together again, I'll turn you out of
doors; remember that.   [*Exit* Harriot.]

[I.ii]   Luckless *and* Mrs. Moneywood.

LUCKLESS.

Discharge all your ill nature on me, madam, but spare poor
Miss Harriot.

MONEYWOOD.

Oh, then it is plain. I have suspected your familiarity a
great while. You are a base man. Is it not enough to stay
three months in my house without paying me a farthing, but   5
you must ruin my child?

LUCKLESS.

I love her as I love my soul. Had I the world, I'd give it
her all.

MONEYWOOD.

But as you happen to have nothing in the world, I desire you
would have nothing to say to her. I suppose you would have   10
settled all your castles in the air. Oh, I wish you had
lodged in one of them instead of my house. Well, I am
resolved, when you are gone away (which I heartily hope
will be very soon) I'll hang over my door in great red letters,
No Lodgings for Poets. Sure, never was such a guest as you have   15
been. My floor is all spoiled with ink, my windows with
verses, and my door has been almost beat down with duns.

LUCKLESS.

Would your house had been beaten down, and everything
but my dear Harriot crushed under it. Must I be your
scolding-stock every morning? And because my pocket is   20
empty, must my head be filled with noise and impertinence?
Naturalists say that all creatures, even the most venomous,
are of some use in the creation; but I'm sure a scolding old
woman is of none, unless she serves in this world as the
devil will in the other, to torment us. And if our torment   25
were to lie in noise, I defy the devil to invent a worse.

MONEYWOOD.

Sir, sir!

LUCKLESS.

Madam, madam! I will attack you at your own weapon.
I'll pay you in your own coin.

MONEYWOOD.

I wish you would pay me in any coin, sir.   30

LUCKLESS.

Pay you! That word is always uppermost in your mouth,
as *Gelt* is in a Dutchman's. Look you, madam, I'll do as
much as a reasonable woman can require; I'll show you all
I have, and give you all I have too, if you please to receive it.

Turns his pockets inside out.

MONEYWOOD.

I will not be used in this manner. No, sir, I will be paid, if 35
there be any such thing as law.

LUCKLESS.

By what law you will put money into my pocket, I don't
know; for I never heard of anyone who got money by the
law but the lawyers. I have told you already, madam, and
I tell you again, that the first money I get shall be yours; 40
and I have great expectations from my play. In the mean-
time, your staying here can be of no service, and you may
possibly drive some fine thoughts out of my head. I must
write a love scene, and your daughter would be properer
company on that occasion than you. 45

MONEYWOOD.

You would act a love scene, I believe, but I shall prevent
you; for I intend to dispose of myself before my daughter.

LUCKLESS.

Dispose of yourself! to whom? to the tallow chandler? You
will never have anything to do with matrimony till Hymen
turns his torch into a tallow candle; then you may be of as 50
much use to him as a fine lady's eyes to Cupid, and may
serve to light young people to bed together.

MONEYWOOD.

You are a vile slanderer. I am not so old, nor so fat, nor so
ugly as you would make me. And 'tis very well known that
I have had very good offers since my last dear husband died, 55
if I would have accepted them. I might have had an attorney
of New Inn, or Mr. Fillpot the exciseman; yes, I had my
choice of two parsons, or a doctor of physic, and yet I
slighted them all. Yes, I slighted them for you.

LUCKLESS.

For me! 60

MONEYWOOD.

Yes, you have seen too visible marks of my passion—too
visible for my reputation.

LUCKLESS.

I have heard very loud tokens of your passion; but I rather
took it for the passion of anger than of love.

---

57. *New Inn*] an Inn of Chancery in Drury Lane.

MONEYWOOD.

Oh, it arose from love! Do but be kind and I'll forgive thee   65
all.

LUCKLESS.

Death! Madam, stand off. If I must be plagued with you, I
had rather you should afflict my eyes than my touch: at a
distance you offend but one sense, but nearer you offend
them all, and I would sooner lose them all than undergo   70
you.

MONEYWOOD.

You shall repent this, sir; remember that. You shall repent
it. I'll show you the revenge of an injured woman.   *Exit.*

LUCKLESS.

I shall never repent anything that rids me of you, madam, I
assure you.   75

[I.iii]   Luckless, Harriot.

HARRIOT.

My dear Harry, I have been waiting an opportunity to
return to you.

LUCKLESS.

My dear Harriot, come to my arms and let me lay my
aching, sick head on thy tender bosom.

HARRIOT.

What's the matter, my dear?   5

LUCKLESS.

I am sick of the most abominable distemper.

HARRIOT.

Heaven forbid! What is it?

LUCKLESS.

Poverty, my love; and your mother is a most excellent nurse.

HARRIOT.

What shall I do for you? My money is all gone, and so are
my clothes; which, when my mother finds out, I shall have as   10
much need of a surgeon as you can have now of a doctor.

LUCKLESS.

No, I would sooner starve, or beg, or steal, or die, than one
hair of my dear Harriot should be hurt. I am armed against
her utmost rage; but for you I fear, for such a spirit as your

mother no Amazon ever possessed before. So, if my present   15
design succeeds, we will leave her together.

HARRIOT.

But if it should fail?

LUCKLESS.

Say, then, my Harriot, would my charmer fly
To the cold climes beneath the polar sky?
Or, armed with love, could she endure to sweat   20
Beneath the sultry, dry equator's heat?
Thirst, hunger, labor, hardship, could she prove,⎫
From conversation of the world remove,   ⎬
And only know the joys of constant love?   ⎭

HARRIOT.

Oh, more than this, my Luckless, would I do.   25
All places are a heaven when with you.
Let me repose but on that faithful breast.
Give me thy love, the world may take the rest.

LUCKLESS.

My dear Harriot! By heaven, thy lips are sweeter than
the honey, and thy temper is yet sweeter than them.   30

Harriot sighs.

Why do you sigh, my sweet?

HARRIOT.

I only wish I were assured of the sincerity of your love.

AIR, Buttered Pease

LUCKLESS.

Does my dearest Harriot ask
  What for love I would pursue?
Would you, charmer, know what task   35
  I would undertake for you?

Ask the bold ambitious, what
  He for honors would achieve;
Or the gay voluptuous, that
  Which he'd not for pleasures give.   40

Ask the miser what he'd do
  To amass excessive gain;

---

33. In O1–3 there is merely a stage direction, "A Song," while the song
itself is printed with the prefatory material; it may have been an after-
thought, as the dialogue runs better without it.

Or the saint, what he'd pursue
    His wished heaven to attain.

These I would attempt, and more.   45
    For oh, my Harriot is to me
All ambition, pleasure store,
    Or what heaven itself can be.

HARRIOT.

Would my dearest Luckless know
    What his constant Harriot can,   50
Her tender love and faith to show
    For her dear, her only man?

Ask the vain coquette what she
    For men's adoration would;
Or from censure to be free,   55
    Ask the vile, censorious prude.

In a coach and six to ride,
    What the mercenary jade;
Or the widow, to be bride
    To a brisk, broad-shouldered blade.   60

All these I would attempt for thee,
    Could I but thy passion fix;
Thy tongue my sole commander be,
    And thy arms my coach and six.

LUCKLESS.

It is unkind in you to doubt it. I wish it was in my power to   65
give you greater proofs, but I will give you the greatest in
my power, which is, to marry you this instant.

HARRIOT.

Then I am easy. But it is better to delay that till our circum-
stances alter. For, remember what you have yourself said in
the song you taught me: 70

Would you the charming Queen of Love
    Invite with you to dwell,
No want your poverty should prove,
    No state your riches tell.

Both her and happiness to hold,   75
    A middle state must please;
They shun the house that shines with gold,
    And that which shines with grease.

MONEYWOOD (*within*).

    Harriot! Harriot!

HARRIOT.

    Hear the dreadful summons. Adieu, my dear. I will take the   80
first opportunity of seeing you again.   [*Exit.*]

LUCKLESS.

    Adieu to my pretty charmer. Go thy ways, for the first of
thy sex. What fool would dangle after, and make himself a
slave to the insolent pride of a mistress when he may find
another with as much good nature as he would wish?   85

[I.iv]   Luckless, Jack.

LUCKLESS.

    So! What news bring you?

JACK.

    An't please your honor, I have been at my lord's, and his
lordship thanks you for the favor you have offered of reading
your play to him, but he has such a prodigious deal of
business, he begs to be excused. I have been with Mr. Keyber   5
too; he made me no answer at all. Mr. Bookweight will be
here immediately.

LUCKLESS.

    Jack!

JACK.

    Sir.

LUCKLESS.

    Fetch my hat hither.   10

JACK.

    It is here, sir.

LUCKLESS.

    Carry it to the pawnbroker's. And, in your way home, call
at the cook's shop. Make haste. So, one way or other I find,
my head must always provide for my belly.   [*Exit* Jack.]

---

    5. *Mr. Keyber*] This Germanic-sounding distortion of Colley Cibber's
name was coined in 1722 to ridicule Cibber's loyal support of the Hano-
verian family. Tory journalists kept the word alive, and even in 1741
Fielding ascribed *Shamela* to Conny Keyber.

[I.v]   Luckless, Witmore.

LUCKLESS.

I am surprised, dear Witmore.

WITMORE.

Dear Harry!

LUCKLESS.

This is kind, indeed, but I do not more wonder at finding a
man in this age who can be a friend to adversity, than that
Fortune should be so much my friend as to direct you to   5
me; for she is a lady I have not been much indebted to
lately.

WITMORE.

She who told me, I assure you, is one you have been indebted to a long while.

LUCKLESS.

Whom do you mean?   10

WITMORE.

One who complains of your unkindness in not visiting her—
Mrs. Lovewood.

LUCKLESS.

Dost thou visit there still, then?

WITMORE.

I throw an idle hour away there sometimes. When I am in an
ill humor I go there and rail, where I am sure to feed it with   15
all the scandal in town. No news writer is more diligent in
procuring intelligence, no bawd in looking after girls with
an uncracked maidenhead, than she in searching out women
with cracked reputations.

LUCKLESS.

The much more infamous office of the two.   20

WITMORE.

Thou art still a favorer of the women, I find.

LUCKLESS.

Aye, the women and the Muses—the high roads to beggary.

WITMORE.

What, art thou not cured of scribbling yet?

LUCKLESS.

No, scribbling is as impossible to cure as the gout.

WITMORE.

And as sure a sign of poverty as the gout of riches. 'Sdeath!   25
In an age of learning and true politeness, where a man might
succeed by his merit, it would be an encouragement. But
now, when party and prejudice carry all before them, when
learning is decried, wit not understood, when the theaters
are puppet shows and the comedians ballad singers, when   30
fools lead the town, would a man think to thrive by his wit?
If you must write, write nonsense, write operas, write entertainments, write *Hurlothrumbos*, set up an *Oratory* and preach
nonsense, and you may meet with encouragement enough.
If you would receive applause, deserve to receive sentence at   35
the Old Bailey; and if you would ride in your coach, deserve
to ride in a cart.

LUCKLESS.

You are warm, my friend.

WITMORE.

It is because I am your friend. I cannot bear to hear the
man I love ridiculed by fools and idiots. To see a fellow who,   40
had he been born a Chinese, had been some low mechanic,
toss up his empty noddle with a scornful disdain of what he
has not understood, and women abusing what they have
neither seen nor read from an unreasonable prejudice to an
honest fellow whom they have not known. If thou wilt write   45
against all these reasons, get a patron, be pimp to some
worthless man of quality, write panegyrics on him, flatter
him with as many virtues as he has vices, and don't pretend
to stand thyself against a tide of prejudice and ill nature
which would have overwhelmed a Plato or a Socrates.   50

LUCKLESS.

I own thy advice is friendly, and I fear too much truth is on
your side. But what would you advise me to do?

---

25 ff.] A likely dramatic model for Witmore's abuse of modern writing
is found in Congreve's *Love for Love* (1695), I.ii, where Scandal dissuades
Valentine from becoming a playwright.

33. *Hurlothrumbos*] *Hurlothrumbo; or, The Super-Natural* (H., Mar. 29,
1729), the fantastic play by Samuel Johnson of Cheshire. See Appendix B.

33. *Oratory*] the first reference to one of the principal targets in the play,
"Orator" Henley. See Appendix B.

35–36. *sentence . . . Bailey*] that is, a sentence as severe as hanging or trans-
portation.

WITMORE.

Thou art a vigorous young fellow—and there are rich widows in town.

LUCKLESS.

But I am already engaged.   55

WITMORE.

Why don't you marry then? For I suppose you are not so mad, to have any engagement with a poor mistress.

LUCKLESS.

Even so, faith, and so heartily that I would not change her for the widow of a Croesus.

WITMORE.

Now thou art undone indeed. Matrimony clenches ruin   60 beyond retrieval. What unfortunate stars wert thou born under? Was it not enough to follow those nine ragged jades the Muses, but you must fasten on some earth-born mistress as poor as them?

LUCKLESS.

Fie, Witmore, thou art grown a churl.   65

WITMORE.

While thou wert happy, I could bear these flights; while thy rooms were furnished and thy clothes whole, I could bear thee. But for a man to preach up love and the Muses in a garret, it would not make me more sick to hear honesty talked of at court, conscience at Westminster, politeness at   70 the university. Nay, I had rather hear women disputing on the mathematics—

[I.vi]   Luckless, Witmore, Bookweight.

LUCKLESS.

Mr. Bookweight, your very humble servant.

BOOKWEIGHT.

I was told, sir, you had particular business with me.

LUCKLESS.

Yes, Mr. Bookweight, I have something to put into your hands. I have a play for you, Mr. Bookweight.

0.1.] Bookweight bears a distinct resemblance to Pamphlet, the book-seller in Farquhar's *Love and a Bottle*, III.ii. For his resemblance to Edmund Curll, see Appendix B.

BOOKWEIGHT.

    Is it accepted, sir?   5

LUCKLESS.

    Not yet.

BOOKWEIGHT.

    Oh, sir, when it is, it will be then time enough to talk about
it. A play, like a bill, is of no value before it is accepted, nor
indeed when it is, very often. This too is a plentiful year of
plays, and they are like nuts: in a plentiful year they are   10
commonly very bad.

LUCKLESS.

    But suppose it were accepted (as you term it), what would
you give me for it? Not that I want money, sir—

BOOKWEIGHT.

    No, sir, certainly. But before I can make any answer I must
read it. I cannot offer anything for what I do not know the   15
value of.

WITMORE.

    That I imagine granted by the players' approbation. For
they are, you know, very great judges.

BOOKWEIGHT.

    Yes, sir, that they are indeed. That they must be allowed to
be, as being men of great learning. But a play which will do   20
for them will not always do for us. There are your acting
plays and your reading plays.

WITMORE.

    I do not understand that distinction.

BOOKWEIGHT.

    Why, sir, your acting play is entirely supported by the merit
of the actor, without any regard to the author at all. In   25
this case, it signifies very little whether there be any sense
in it or no. Now your reading play is of a different stamp
and must have wit and meaning in it. These latter I call
your substantive, as being able to support themselves.
The former are your adjective, as what require the buffoon-   30
ery and gestures of an actor to be joined to them to show
their signification.

    9–10. *plentiful . . . plays*] an accurate observation, since about a dozen
from the 1729–1730 season had preceded *The Author's Farce* into print.

LUCKLESS.

Very learnedly defined, truly, Mr. Bookweight.

BOOKWEIGHT.

I hope I have not had so much learning go through my
hands without leaving some in my head.   35

LUCKLESS.

Well, but Mr. Bookweight, I hope you will advance something.

BOOKWEIGHT.

Why, had you a great reputation I might venture. But truly,
for young beginners it is a very great hazard. For indeed
the reputation of the author carries the greatest sway in these   40
affairs. The town have been so fond of some authors that
they have run them up to infallibility, and would have
applauded them even against their senses.

WITMORE.

And who but a madman would write in such an age?

LUCKLESS.

'Sdeath, Witmore! 'Tis cruel to insult my misfortunes.   45

WITMORE.

I would cure them, and that is not to be done by lenitives.

BOOKWEIGHT.

I am of that gentleman's opinion. I do think writing is the
silliest thing a man can undertake.

LUCKLESS.

'Tis strange you should say so, who live by it.

BOOKWEIGHT.

Live by it! Ah, if you had lost as much by writers as I have   50
done, you would be of my opinion.

LUCKLESS.

But we are losing time. Will you advance fifty guineas on
my play?

BOOKWEIGHT.

No, nor fifty shillings, I assure you.

LUCKLESS.

'Sdeath, sir! Do you beat me down at this rate?   55

---

46. *lenitives*] soothing medicines.
52. *fifty guineas*] an exorbitant demand, since few established playwrights could hope to realize as much from a single work.

BOOKWEIGHT.

Sir, I would not give you fifty farthings. Fifty guineas,
indeed! Your name is well worth that.

Jack *enters.*

LUCKLESS.

Jack, take this worthy gentleman and kick him downstairs.

BOOKWEIGHT.

Sir, I shall make you repent this.

JACK.

Come, sir, will you please to brush?   60

BOOKWEIGHT.

Help! Murder! I'll have the law of you, sir.

LUCKLESS.

Ha, ha, ha!   [*Exeunt* Bookweight, Jack.]

[I.vii]   Luckless, Witmore, Mrs. Moneywood.

MONEYWOOD.

What noise is this? It is a very fine thing truly, Mr. Luckless, that you will make these uproars in my house.

LUCKLESS.

If you dislike it, it is in your power to drown a much greater.
Do you but speak, madam, and I am sure no one will be
heard but yourself.   5

MONEYWOOD.

Very well, indeed! Fine reflections on my character! Sir, sir,
all the neighbors know that I have been as quiet a woman as
any in the parish. I had no noises in my house till you came.
We were the Family of Love. But you have been a nuisance
to the whole neighborhood. While you had money my doors   10
were thundered at every morning at four and five, and since
you have had none, my walls have echoed nothing but your
noise and your poetry. Then there's the rascal your man.

---

60. *to brush*] to get out, make a hasty exit.
[I.vii]
9. *Family of Love*] the phrase may glance obliquely at the Familists,
founded in the sixteenth century by Henrick Niclaes, and a target for
dramatic satire in earlier times, as in Thomas Middleton's *The Family of
Love* (*c.* 1606). Swift in *The Mechanical Operation of the Spirit* (1704) mentions it
as a fanatic group still existing, but in *Jonathan Wild*, IV, 16, Fielding uses
the phrase for a harmonious family group, without apparent satiric
overtones.

But I'll pay the dog, I'll scour him.   (*To* Witmore.)   Sir,
I am glad you are a witness to his abuses of me.   15

WITMORE.

I am a witness indeed, madam, how unjustly he has abused
you.

Jack [*enters and*] *whispers.*

LUCKLESS.

Witmore, you'll excuse me a moment.   *Exeunt* Luckless, Jack.

[I.viii]   Mrs. Moneywood, Witmore.

MONEYWOOD.

Yes, sir. And sir, a man that has never shown one the color of
his money.

WITMORE.

Very hard, truly. How much may he be in your debt, pray?
Because he has ordered me to pay you.

MONEYWOOD.

Ah, sir, I wish he had.   5

WITMORE.

I am serious, I assure you.

MONEYWOOD.

I am very glad to hear it, sir. Here is the bill as we settled
it this very morning. I always thought indeed Mr. Luckless
had a good deal of honesty in his principles. Any man may
be unfortunate, but I knew when he had money I should   10
have it. I never was in any fear for my money, for my part.

WITMORE.

There, madam, is your money on the table. Please to write
a receipt only.

MONEYWOOD.

Sir, I give you a great many thanks. There, sir, is the
receipt. Well, if Mr. Luckless was but a little soberer, I   15
should like him for a lodger exceedingly, for I must say I
think him a very pleasant good-natured man.

[I.ix]   Luckless *returns.*

LUCKLESS.

Those are words I never heard out of that mouth before.

MONEYWOOD.

Ha, Ha, Ha! You are pleased to be merry.

LUCKLESS.

Why Witmore, thou hast the faculty opposite to that of a witch, and canst lay a tempest. I should have as soon imagined one man could have stopped a cannon ball in its full force as her tongue, and I believe she may be heard as far. Were she to roar forth a summons to a town, it would have more effect on the governor than a volley of artillery.

MONEYWOOD.

Ha, ha, ha!

WITMORE.

Luckless, good morrow. I will see you again soon.   10

LUCKLESS.

Witmore, I am yours.   [*Exit* Witmore.]

[I.x]   Luckless, Mrs. Moneywood.

MONEYWOOD.

Well, Mr. Luckless, you are a comical man, to give one such a character to a stranger.

LUCKLESS.

The company is gone, madam; and now, like true man and wife, we may fall to abusing one another as fast as we please.

MONEYWOOD.

Abuse me as you will, so you pay me, sir.   5

LUCKLESS.

'Sdeath, madam, I will pay you.

MONEYWOOD.

Nay, sir, I do not ask it before it is due. I don't question your payment at all. If you were to stay in my house this quarter of a year, as I hope you will, I should not ask you for a farthing.   10

LUCKLESS [*aside*].

Tol, lol, lol. But I shall have her begin with her passion immediately, and I had rather feel the highest effects of her rage than the lightest of her love.

MONEYWOOD.

But why did you choose to surprise me with my money? Why did you not tell me you'd pay me?   15

LUCKLESS.

Why have I not told you?

MONEYWOOD.

Yes, you told me of a play and stuff, and you never told me you would order a gentleman to pay me. Well, you have comical ways with you, but you have honesty in the bottom, and I'm sure the gentleman himself will own I gave you that   20 character.

LUCKLESS [*aside*].

Oh! I smell you now. —You see, madam, I am better than my word to you. Did he pay it you in gold or silver?

MONEYWOOD.

All pure gold.

LUCKLESS.

I have a vast deal of silver within. Will you do me the favor   25 of taking it in silver? That may be of use to you in the shop too.

MONEYWOOD.

Anything to oblige you, sir.

LUCKLESS.

Jack, bring out the great bag number one. Please to tell the money, madam, on that table.   30

MONEYWOOD (*tells the money*).

It's easily told. Heaven knows there's not so much on't.

Enter Jack.
When Jack *enters*, Luckless *gets between*
Mrs. Moneywood *and the table.*

JACK.

Sir, the bag is so heavy I cannot bring it in.

LUCKLESS.

Why then, come and help to thrust a heavier bag out.

MONEYWOOD.

What do you mean, sir?

LUCKLESS.

Only to pay you in my bedchamber.   35

MONEYWOOD.

Villain, dog, I'll swear a robbery and have you hanged. Rogues, villains!

LUCKLESS (*shuts the door*).

Be as noisy as you please. Jack, call a coach and, d'ye hear, get up behind it and attend me.   [*Exeunt.*]

ACT II

A tavern.
Luckless, Marplay, Sparkish.

LUCKLESS (*reads*).

> *Then hence my sorrows, hence my every fear,*
> *No matter where, so we are blessed together.*
> *With thee, the barren rocks, where not one step*
> *Of human race lies printed in the snow,*
> *Look lovely as the smiling infant spring.*   5

MARPLAY (*yawning*).

Will you please to read that again, sir?

LUCKLESS (*reads again*).

MARPLAY.

> *Then hence my sorrow* ... Horror is a much better word, in my opinion. And then in the second line—will you please to read it again?

LUCKLESS.

> *No matter where, so we are blessed together.*   10

MARPLAY.

In my opinion it would be better so:
> *No matter where, so somewhere we're together.*

Where is the question, somewhere is the answer. Read on, sir.

LUCKLESS (*reads on*).

> *With thee,* etc.   15

MARPLAY.

I could alter those lines to a much better idea.
> *With thee, the barren blocks* (that is, trees) *where not a bit*
> *Of human face is painted on the bark,*
> *Look green as Covent Garden in the spring.*

LUCKLESS.

Green as Covent Garden?   20

0.1.] Marplay and Sparkish are Colley Cibber and Robert Wilks, two of the triumvirate managing Drury Lane; see Appendix B. The third member, Barton Booth, is ignored; he and Fielding were on good terms, and illness prevented Booth from being very active in theatrical affairs after 1728.

MARPLAY.

Yes, Covent Garden Market, where they sell greens.

LUCKLESS.

Monstrous! Sir, I must ask your pardon, I cannot consent to such an alteration. It is downright nonsense.

MARPLAY (*rising from the table*).

Sir, it will not do, and so I would not have you think any more of it. 25

SPARKISH.

No, no, no. It will not do.

LUCKLESS.

What faults do you find?

MARPLAY.

Sir, there is nothing in it that pleases me, so I am sure there is nothing in it that will please the town.

SPARKISH.

There is nothing in it that will please the town. 30

LUCKLESS.

Methinks you should find some particular fault.

MARPLAY.

Truly, sir, it is so full of faults that the eye of my judgment is so distracted with the variety of objects that it cannot fix on any.

SPARKISH.

No, no, no—cannot fix on any. 35

MARPLAY.

In short, there is not one good thing in it from the beginning to the end.

LUCKLESS.

Some who have read it think otherwise.

MARPLAY.

Let them think as they please. I'm sure we are the best judges. 40

SPARKISH.

Yes, yes, we are the best judges.

LUCKLESS.

Could you convince me of any fault, I would amend it. But you argue in plays as the Pope does in religion or the Aristotelists in philosophy: you maintain your hypothesis by an *ipse dicit*. 45

MARPLAY.

I don't understand you hard words, sir. But I think it is very hard if a man who has been so long in a trade as I have should not understand the value of his merchandise, should not know what goods will best please the town. —Come, Sparkish, will you go to Tom's?   50

LUCKLESS.

Fare ye well, gentlemen. May another play do you more service.   [*Exit.*]

[II.ii]   Marplay, Sparkish.

MARPLAY.

Ha, ha, ha!

SPARKISH.

What dost think of the play?

MARPLAY.

It may be a very good one for aught I know; but I know the author has no interest.

SPARKISH.

Give me interest, and rat the play.   5

MARPLAY.

Rather rat the play which has no interest. Interest sways as much in the theater as at court, and you know it is not always the companion of merit in either.

SPARKISH.

But pray, Mr. Marplay, what was the reason of that extra-ordinary demand of yours upon the office?   10

MARPLAY.

Truly, sir, it was for the good of the office. Some of it was given to puffs to cry up our new plays, and one half guinea to Mr. Scribler for a panegyrical essay in the newspaper, with

---

50. *Tom's*] Tom's Coffee House, No. 17 Russell Street, Covent Garden, a favorite rendezvous and gambling place for actors and people of fashion.
[II.ii]
4. *interest*] influence.
10. *demand . . . office*] withdrawal of money from the theater business office.

some other such services. But have you seen my new entertainment practised, *Cuckolds All a Row*? 15

SPARKISH.

No.

MARPLAY.

I will affirm this, that it is the best thing that has ever
appeared on the stage. I don't know whether I shall not lay
the pit and boxes together at half a guinea a seat.

SPARKISH.

I would not advise that, for the town grumbles at our raising 20
the prices as we have done.

MARPLAY.

Rat the town. Let them grumble, I'm sure they will not stay
away. For their hisses, they have no more effect on me than
music would have on an owl, or the curses of an undone
client on an attorney. I have been used to them, and any 25
man who loves hissing may have his three shillings' worth at
me whenever he pleases. [*Exeunt.*]

[II.iii]   *A room in Mr. Bookweight's house.*
            Dash, Blotpage, Quibble *writing at several tables.*

DASH.

Pox on't, I'm as dull as an ox though I have not a bit of one
within me; I have not dined these two days, and yet my head
is as heavy as any alderman's or lord's. I carry about me
symbols of all the elements: my head is as heavy as water,
my pockets are light as air, my appetite is as hot as fire, and 5
my coat is as dirty as earth.

---

15. *Cuckolds All a Row*] The phrase is from an old song, here used to
reflect ironically on Cibber's virtuous entertainment, the pastoral ballad
opera *Love in a Riddle* (D.L., Jan 7, 1729), which was hissed off the stage at
its second performance. Its damnation was assured when Gay's *Polly* was
banned, and hostile journals saw to it that Cibber's ballad opera should not
succeed when Gay's was not allowed. This disaster for Cibber is again
exploited in III, 154, 504.

18–19. *lay . . . together*] charge the same price for pit as for boxes, a
frequent practice at benefits or other special performances when a full
house was expected; usually this would mean a price of 5*s*. (as for *The
Author's Farce* after its success was assured), though the half guinea Marplay
suggests was sometimes charged.

BLOTPAGE.

    Lend me your Bysshe, Mr. Dash; I want a rhyme for wind.

DASH.

    Why there! blind, and kind, and behind, and find, and
mind. It is one of the easiest terminations imaginable; I have
had it four times in a page.   10

BLOTPAGE.

    Devil take the first inventor of rhyming, I say. Your business
is much easier, Mr. Dash. Well, of all the places in my
master's gift I should most like to be clerk of the ghosts and
murders. You have nothing to do but to put a set of
terrible words together in the title page.   15

DASH.

    The business is easy enough, but it is at a very low ebb
now. No, Mr. Quibble there, as clerk of the libels, would
have the best place, were it not that few men ever sat in his
chair long without standing on an odd sort of stool in the
street to be gaped at an hour or two by the mob.   20

QUIBBLE.

    We act on different principles, Mr. Dash: 'tis your business
to promise more than you perform, and mine to promise less.

BLOTPAGE.

    Pshaw! Thy business is to perform nothing at all.

DASH.

    It becomes an author to be diffusive in his title page. A
title page is to a book what a fine neck is to a woman, there-   25
fore ought to be the most regarded as it is the part which is
viewed before the purchase.

AIR, *Ye Commons and Peers*

BLOTPAGE.   How uphappy's the fate
                To live by one's pate
                And be forced to write hackney for bread!   30

---

    7. *Bysshe*] Edward Bysshe, *The Art of English Poetry* (1702), with "A
Dictionary of Rhymes" as one of its main divisions.

    19–20. *an odd . . . street*] the pillory.

    28–46.] The song, like the Luckless–Harriot duet in Act I, is printed
with the prefatory material and its place here merely indicated by a stage
direction. In the 1734 revision (probably because of changes in cast) it is
given to Dash.

An author's a joke
To all manner of folk
Wherever he pops up his head, his head,
Wherever he pops up his head.

Though he mount on that hack,   35
Old Pegasus' back,
And of Helicon drink till he burst,
Yet a curse of those streams,
Poetical dreams,
They never can quench one's thirst, etc.   40

Ah, how should he fly
On fancy so high
When his limbs are in durance and hold?
Or how should he charm
With genius so warm,   45
When his poor naked body's acold, etc.

[II.iv]   *To them* Bookweight.

BOOKWEIGHT.

Fie upon it, gentlemen! What, not at your pens? Do you
consider, Mr. Quibble, that it is above a fortnight since your
Letter from a Friend in the Country was published? Is it not
high time for an Answer to come out? At this rate, before
your Answer in printed your Letter will be forgot. I love to   5
keep a controversy up warm. I have had authors who have
writ a pamphlet in the morning, answered it in the afternoon, and compromised the matter at night.

QUIBBLE.

Sir, I will be as expeditious as possible.

BOOKWEIGHT.

Well, Mr. Dash, have you done that murder yet?   10

DASH.

Yes, sir, the murder is done. I am only about a few moral
reflections to place before it.

BOOKWEIGHT.

Very well. Then let me have the ghost finished by this day
sevennight.

DASH.

 What sort of a ghost would you have, sir? The last was a   15
pale one.

BOOKWEIGHT.

 Then let this be a bloody one. Mr. Blotpage, what have your
lucubrations produced? (*Reads.*) "Poetical advice to a
certain———from a certain———on a certain———
from a certain———." Very good! I will say, Mr. Blot-   20
page writes as good a dash as any man in Europe.

[II.v]   *To them* Index.

BOOKWEIGHT.

 So, Mr. Index, what news with you?

INDEX.

 I have brought my bill, sir.

BOOKWEIGHT.

 What's here?— "For adapting the motto of *Risum teneatis
amici* to a dozen pamphlets at sixpence per each, six shillings.
For *Omnia vincit amor et nos cedamus amori*, sixpence. For   5
Difficile est satyram non scribere, sixpence." Hum, hum, hum.
Ah. "A sum total, for thirty-six Latin mottos, eighteen
shillings; ditto English, seven, one shilling and ninepence;
ditto Greek, four, one shilling." —Why, friend, are your
Latin mottos dearer than your Greek?   10

INDEX.

 Yes marry are they, sir. For as nobody now understands
Greek, so I may use any sentence in that language to
whatsoever purpose I please.

BOOKWEIGHT.

 You shall have your money immediately. And pray remember that I must have two Latin sedition mottos and one   15
Greek moral motto for pamphlets by tomorrow morning.

QUIBBLE.

 I want two Latin sentences, sir, one for page the fourth in

 3–6. *Risum . . . scribere*] Even Bookweight might have objected that
Index's quotations were a little shopworn: (1) Horace, *Ars poetica*, 5, "Could
you refrain from laughing, my friends?"; (2) Virgil, *Eclogues*, X, 69, "Love
conquers all, and we must yield to love" (Dryden); (2) Juvenal, I, 30, "It
is hard not to write satire."

the praise of virtue, and the other for page the tenth in the
praise of beauty.

BOOKWEIGHT.

Let me have those too.   20

INDEX.

Sir, I shall take care to provide them.   [*Exit.*]

[II.vi]   Bookweight, Dash, Blotpage, Quibble, Scarecrow.

SCARECROW.

Sir, I have brought you a libel against the ministry.

BOOKWEIGHT.

Sir, I shall not take anything against them— (*aside*) for I
have two in the press already.

SCARECROW.

Then, sir, I have another in defense of them.

BOOKWEIGHT.

Sir, I never take anything in defense of power.   5

SCARECROW.

I have a translation of Virgil's *Aeneid*, with notes on it.

BOOKWEIGHT.

That, sir, is what I do not care to venture on. You may try
by subscription if you please, but I would not advise you,
for that bubble is almost down. People begin to be afraid
of authors since they have writ and acted like stockjobbers.   10
So to oblige a young beginner, I don't care if I print it at
my own expense.

SCARECROW.

But pray, sir, at whose expense shall I eat?

BOOKWEIGHT.

That's an empty question.

SCARECROW.

It comes from an empty stomach, I'm sure.   15

BOOKWEIGHT.

From an empty head, I'm afraid. Are there not a thousand
ways for a man to get his bread by?

SCARECROW.

I wish you would put me into one.

---

10. *stockjobbers*] brokers who trade in stocks on their own behalf.

BOOKWEIGHT.

Why then, sir, I would advise you to come and take your seat
at my tables. Here will be everything that is necessary pro-   20
vided for you. I am as great a friend to learning as the
Dutch are to trade. No one can want bread with me who will
earn it. Besides, a translator will be of use to me, for my
last is in Newgate for shoplifting. The rogue had gotten a
trick of translating out of the shops as well as out of the   25
languages.

SCARECROW.

I prefer anything to starving.

BOOKWEIGHT.

Then, sir, if you please to throw by your hat, which you will
have no more use for, and take up your pen.

SCARECROW.

But, sir, I am afraid I am not qualified for a translator.   30

BOOKWEIGHT.

How, not qualified?

SCARECROW.

No, sir, I understand no language but my own.

BOOKWEIGHT.

What, and translate Virgil?

SCARECROW.

Alas, sir, I translated him out of Dryden.

BOOKWEIGHT.

Not qualified! If I was an emperor thou shouldst be my   35
prime minister. Thou art as well versed in thy trade as if
thou hadst labored in my garret these ten years. Let me tell
you, friend, you will have more occasion for invention than
learning here: you will be sometimes obliged to translate
books out of all languages (especially French) which were   40
never printed in any language whatsoever.

SCARECROW.

Your trade abounds in mysteries.

BOOKWEIGHT.

The study of bookselling is as difficult as the law, and there
are as many tricks in the one as the other. Sometimes we
give a foreign name to our own labor, and sometimes we put   45
our own names to the labor of others. Then as the lawyers

have John-a-Nokes and Tom-a-Stiles, so we have Messieurs
Moore near St. Paul's and Smith near the Royal Exchange.

[II.vii]   *To them* Luckless.

LUCKLESS.

Mr. Bookweight, your servant. Who can form to himself
an idea more amiable than of a man at the head of so many
patriots working for the benefit of their country?

BOOKWEIGHT.

Truly, sir, I believe it is an idea more agreeable to you
than that of a gentleman in the Crown Office paying thirty   5
or forty guineas for abusing an honest tradesman.

LUCKLESS.

Pshaw, that was only jocosely done, and a man who lives by
wit must not be angry at a jest. Besides, the law has been
your enemy, and you would not fly to an enemy for succor.

BOOKWEIGHT.

Sir, I will use my enemy as I would my friend, for my own   10
ends. But pray, sir, what has brought you hither? If you
have a mind to compromise the matter, I had rather have a
little of your money than that the lawyers should have a
great deal.

LUCKLESS.

Hast thou dealt in paper so long, and talk of money to a   15

---

47. *John-a-Nokes and Tom-a-Styles*] fictitious names used in law warrants.
Fielding is suggesting that Bookweight used fictitious publisher's imprints
as the lawyers used these names: "A. Moore near St. Paul's" about this
time published a number of works of which Curll was at least part owner,
and "[Elizabeth?] Smith near the Royal Exchange," although less easy to
trace, was probably also a front for him.
[II.vii]
5. *Crown Office*] "Here Informations may be laid for Offences and Mis-
demeanors at Common Law, as for *Batteries, Conspiracies, Libelling, Nusances,
Contempt, Seditious Words*, &c. wherein the Offender is liable to pay a Fine
to the King. . . . When a *Battery* is committed privately, so the Person receiving it can make no Proof thereof by Witnesses at Law; it is usual to
bring an Information in this Office, where the Party may be a Witness for
the King, it being his Suit" (Giles Jacob, *A New Law Dictionary*, 8th ed.,
1762). Bookweight is threatening Luckless because of his violent ejection
from Luckless's lodgings in I.vi.

modern author? You might as well have talked Latin or Greek to him. I have brought you paper, sir.

BOOKWEIGHT.

That is not bringing me money, I own. But it shall not be taking away money, sir, for I will have nothing to do with your paper or you either.   20

LUCKLESS.

Why prithee, man, I have not brought you a play—nor a sermon.

BOOKWEIGHT.

Have you brought me an opera?

LUCKLESS.

You may call it an opera if you will, but I call it a puppet show.   25

BOOKWEIGHT.

A puppet show!

LUCKLESS.

Aye, a puppet show, and is to be played this night in the Haymarket playhouse.

BOOKWEIGHT.

A puppet show in a playhouse!

LUCKLESS.

What have been all the playhouses a long time but puppet   30
shows?

BOOKWEIGHT.

Why, I don't know but it may succeed. At least, I had rather venture on a thing of that nature than a regular play. So if you please to come in, if I can make a bargain with you I will. Gentlemen, you may go to dinner.   [*Exeunt.*]   35

[II.viii]   *The street.*
     Enter Jack Pudding, *Drummer, and Mob. The drum ceasing—*

JACK PUDDING.

This is to give notice to all gentlemen, ladies, and others, that at the playhouse opposite to the Opera in the Hay-

---

1. S.P. *Jack Pudding*] The prefix *Har.* in O1–3 is the only error in the text that cannot be simply explained. It is remotely possible that Fielding once thought of involving Harriot in Luckless's venture (as she indeed is in the revised version).

market this evening will be performed the whole puppet
show called *The Pleasures of the Town,* in which will be
shown the whole Court of Dullness, with abundance of sing-   5
ing and dancing and several other entertainments; also the
comical and diverting humors of Somebody and Nobody,
Punch and his wife Joan; to be performed by living figures,
some of them six foot high, beginning exactly at seven
o'clock. God save the King!   *Drum beats.* [*Exeunt.*]   10

[II.ix]   Witmore *with a paper,* Luckless *meeting.*

WITMORE.

Oh, Luckless, I am overjoyed at meeting you. Here, take
this paper and you will be discouraged from writing, I
warrant you.

LUCKLESS.

What is it? Oh, one of my playbills.

WITMORE.

One of thy playbills?   5

LUCKLESS.

Even so, sir. I have taken the advice you gave me this
morning.

WITMORE.

Explain.

LUCKLESS.

Why, I had some time since given this puppet show of mine
to be rehearsed and the actors were all perfect in their parts.   10
But we happened to dissent about some particulars, and I
had a design to have given it over; till having my play
refused by Marplay and Sparkish, I sent for the managers of
the house in a passion, joined issue with them, and this very
evening it is to be acted.   15

---

5. *Dullness*] Luckless's entertainment actually represents the Court of
Nonsense, recalling Dryden's *MacFlecknoe*; Pope in the *Dunciad* greatly
expanded Dryden's concept and changed "Nonsense" to the more subtle
term "Dullness." Fielding may here be expressing his indebtedness to Pope
or he may have made a slip of the pen; the revised version here reads
"Court of Nonsense."

9. *six foot high*] Puppet-show notices bragged of the size of the puppets
"four or five feet high."

WITMORE.

Well, I wish you success.

LUCKLESS.

Where are you going?

WITMORE.

Anywhere but to hear you damned, which I must if I were to
go to your puppet show. I tell you the town is prejudiced
against you and they will damn you, whether you deserve   20
it or no. If they should laugh till they burst, the moment
they knew you were the author they would change their faces
and swear they never laughed at all.

LUCKLESS.

Pshaw, I can't believe thee.

WITMORE.

'Sdeath! I have heard sense run down and seen idiotism,   25
downright idiotism triumph so often, that I could almost
think of wit and folly as Mr. Hobbes does of moral good and
evil, that there are no such things.

LUCKLESS.

Well, indulge me in this trial, and I assure thee if it be
successless it shall be the last.   30

WITMORE.

On that condition I will. But should the torrent run against
you, I shall be a fashionable friend and hiss with the rest.

LUCKLESS.

No, a man who could do so unfashionable and so generous
a thing as Mr. Witmore did this morning—

WITMORE.

In return, will you grant me a favor?   35

LUCKLESS.

Do you doubt it?

WITMORE.

Never mention it to me more. I will now to the pit.

LUCKLESS.

And I behind the scenes.   [*Exeunt.*]

[II.x]   *Mrs. Moneywood's.*
                   Mrs. Moneywood *and* Harriot.

HARRIOT.

It is very hard, madam, that you will not suffer me at least

to indulge myself in grief, that it is not enough to tear me
from the man I love but I must have my ears eternally cursed
with hearing him abused.

MONEYWOOD.

On monstrous! Love a puppet-show fellow!   5

HARRIOT.

His misfortunes may lessen him in the eye of the world,
but they shall never lessen him in mine. Nay, I love him for
them.

MONEYWOOD.

You have not a drop of my blood in you. Love a man for his
misfortune! Hussy, to be poor and unfortunate are crimes.   10
Riches are the only recommendations to people of sense
of both sexes, and a coach and six is one of the cardinal
virtues.

HARRIOT.

I despise it and the fool who was born to it. No, give me
the man who, thrown naked upon the world like my dear   15
Luckless, can make his way through it by his merit and
virtuous industry.

MONEYWOOD.

Virtuous industry! A very virtuous, industrious gentleman,
truly. He hath robbed me of a few guineas today or so, but he
is a very virtuous man no doubt.   20

HARRIOT.

He hath only borrowed what you know he will repay. You
know he is honest.

MONEYWOOD.

I am no more satisfied of his honesty that you can be of his
love.

HARRIOT.

Which I am sure he hath given me sufficient proofs of.   25

MONEYWOOD.

Proofs! Oh the villain! Hath he given you proofs of love?

HARRIOT.

All that a modest woman can require.

MONEYWOOD.

If he hath given you all a modest woman can require, I am
afraid he has given you more than a modest woman should
take. Because he hath been so good a lodger, I suppose I   30

shall have some more of the family to keep. It is probable
I may live to see half a dozen grandsons of mine in Grub
Street.

Enter Jack.

MONEYWOOD.

So, rascal, what's become of your master?

JACK.

Oh, madam, I am frightened out of my wits. 35

MONEYWOOD, HARRIOT.

What's the matter?

JACK.

There's the strangest sort of a man below inquiring after my
master that ever was seen.

MONEYWOOD.

What, I suppose a sort of bailiff?

JACK.

Oh, madam, I fancy it is the Man in the Moon, or some 40
monster. There are five hundred people at the door looking
at him. He is dressed up in nothing but ruffles and cabbage
nets.

MONEYWOOD.

This is either some trick of his to catch me, or some trick
of a bailiff to catch him. However, I'll go sift out the bottom 45
of it. Come, show me where he is.

HARRIOT.

Heavens protect my dear Luckless. [*Exeunt.*]

ACT III

The playhouse.
Enter Luckless *as master of the show, and* Player.

LUCKLESS.

It's very surprising that after I have been at all this expense
and trouble to set up my things in your house you should
desire me to recant; and now too, when the spectators are all
assembled and will either have the show or their money.

PLAYER.

It is beneath the dignity of the stage.   5

LUCKLESS.

That may be; so is all farce, and yet you see a farce brings
more company to a house than the best play that ever was
writ, for this age would allow Tom Durfey a better poet than
Congreve or Wycherley. Who would not then rather eat by
his nonsense than starve by his wit? The lodgings of wits   10
have long been in the air, and air must be their food
nowadays.

PLAYER.

I am not the first indeed that has disgraced the stage.

LUCKLESS.

And I heartily wish you may be the last, and that my

The running head changes to *The Pleasures of the Town* for all of Act III,
though strictly speaking this entertainment does not begin until l. 45.
Though it is interrupted by Murdertext, Fielding thought of the entertainment as continuing until Witmore's entrance at line 767, since Luckless's
speeches from the beginning of the act to this point are headed *Mast.* (i.e.,
master of the show). The setting is the Little Theatre in the Haymarket,
and Luckless's show has no other audience than that actually assembled
in the auditorium. *The Beggar's Opera*, with its introductory dialogue
between the Beggar and the Player, suggested that between Luckless as
Master of the Show and the Player. Both scenes were played on the fore-
stage in front of the closed curtain, both pretend that the entertainment to
follow was not originally designed for a legitimate playhouse, and both end
with the supposed playwright's request to the orchestra to begin the overture. In short, both are conceived as prologues which will prepare the
audience for a dramatic innovation.

8. *Durfey*] Although once sprightly enough to amuse Charles II, Thomas
Durfey (1653–1723), playwright and song collector, had become generally
regarded as a representatative of dullness by the time Fielding was writing.

puppet show may expel farce and opera as they have done   15
tragedy and comedy.

PLAYER.

But hark you, friend, how came you to call this performance
of yours a puppet show?

LUCKLESS.

You must know, sir, that it was originally designed to be
played by real puppets, till a friend of mine observing the   20
success of some things in town, advised me to bring it on the
stage. I had offered it to the old house, but they say nothing
but your fine sense, such plays as *Caesar in Egypt*, will go
down there.

PLAYER.

But what is the design or plot? For I could make neither   25
head nor tail of it, for my part.

LUCKLESS.

Why sir, the Goddess of Nonsense is to fall in love with the
ghost of Signior Opera.

PLAYER.

Fall in love with a ghost, ha, ha, ha!

LUCKLESS.

Aye, sir. You must know that the scene is laid on the other   30
side of the River Styx, so all the people of the play are
ghosts.

---

20. *real puppets*] Since it was often charged that actors had become mere
puppets, it is hardly unexpected to find them taking puppet parts: live
Punches turned up, for example, at Lincoln's Inn Fields when Shaw acted
Punch in *The Cheats* in 1717 and *The Jealous Doctor* in 1718; a Drury Lane
production of *The Escapes of Harlequin* in 1722 offered two Punches as well
as two "Punch Women." Still, there was little precedent for a complete
puppet show performed by living actors, although a lost play by Thomas
Sheridan, *Punch Turned School-Master*, produced in Dublin in 1721, was such.
Whether Fielding knew Sheridan's work or not, he probably instructed his
actors to mimic the sounds and movements of puppets, as Sheridan had done.

22. *old house*] Drury Lane, the oldest theatrical structure in London.

23. *Caesar in Egypt*] Cibber's dramatization of the Caesar and Cleopatra
story appeared at Drury Lane in 1724 and was immediately ridiculed
without mercy.

30–31. *other . . . Styx*] Lucian's *Dialogues of the Dead* (perhaps with assistance from the *Frogs* of Aristophanes) are the chief influence here, but
current theatrical fashion had its share. Creators of contemporary pantomime were extremely fond of the infernal regions, and by 1730 it was anything but a novelty to see Charon on the London stage.

PLAYER.

This marrying of ghosts is a new doctrine, friend.

LUCKLESS.

So much the likelier to please. Though I can't say but I
took the hint of this thing from the old house, who observing   35
that everyone could not see the real coronation brought a
representation of it upon their stage. So, sir, since everyone
has not time or opportunity to visit all the diversions of the
town, I have brought most of them together in one. But
come, it is time to begin. I think we will have an overture,   40
though ours be not a regular opera.

PLAYER.

By all means an overture.

LUCKLESS.

If you please, sir, you shall sit down by me. Play away.

[Music.]

LUCKLESS.

Gentlemen, the first thing I present you with is Punchinello.

The curtain drawn discovers Punch in a great chair.
Punch sings.

AIR I, Whilst the Town's Brimful of Folly

PUNCH.   Whilst the town's brimful of farces,   45
                          Flocking whilst we see her asses
                             Thick as grapes upon a bunch,
                          Critics, whilst you smile on madness,
                          And more stupid, solemn sadness,
                             Sure you will not frown on Punch.   50

LUCKLESS.

The next is Punch's wife Joan.

---

36. *real coronation.*] The coronation of George II on October 11, 1727,
prompted a revival of Shakespeare's *Henry VIII* at Drury Lane featuring the
coronation of Anne Bullen, which Rich promptly burlesqued in a pantomime called *Harlequin Anne Bullen. Mist's Weekly Journal* for Jan. 6, 1728,
notes "that in a certain Alley in Wapping during these Holidays the
Coronation of *Anna Bullen* has been represented by *Punch*'s Company of
Actors. . . . "

44.] Luckless in his role as "Master" recalls Leatherhead in Ben Jonson's
Bartholomew Fair (1614).

Enter Joan.

JOAN.

> What can ail my husband? He is continually humming
> tunes, though his voice be only fit to warble at Hog's Norton
> where the pigs would accompany it with organs. I was in
> hopes death would have stopped his mouth at last. But he   55
> keeps his old harmonious humor even in the shades.

PUNCH.

> Be not angry, dear Joan. Orpheus obtained his wife from the
> shades by charming Pluto with his music.

JOAN.

> Sirrah, sirrah, should Pluto hear you sing, you could expect
> no less punishment than Tantalus has; nay, the waters   60
> would be brought above your mouth to stop it.

PUNCH.

> Truly, madam, I don't wish the same success Orpheus met
> with; could I gain my own liberty, the devil might have
> you with all my heart.

AIR II

> Joan, Joan, Joan has a thundering tongue,   65
> And Joan, Joan, Joan is a bold one.
> > How happy is he
> > Who from wedlock is free,
> For who'd have a wife to scold one?

JOAN.

> Punch, Punch, Punch, prithee think of your hunch,   70
> Prithee look at your great strutting belly.
> > Sirrah, if you dare
> > War with me declare,
> I will beat your fat guts to a jelly.

Here they dance.

AIR III, *Bobbing Joan*

PUNCH.

> Joan, you are the plague of my life.   75
> A rope would be welcomer than such a wife.

JOAN.

> Punch, your merits had you but shared,
> Your neck had been longer by half a yard.

---

53. *Hog's Norton*] Hock Norton, a village in Oxfordshire proverbial for
boorishness and for the music of its pigs.

64.1. *AIR II*] The Dublin edition of 1730 identifies this as "The First of
August."

PUNCH.	Ugly witch.	
JOAN.	Son of a bitch.	80
BOTH.	Would you were hanged or drowned in a ditch.	

Here they dance again.

PUNCH. Since we hate, like people in vogue,
    Let us call not bitch and rogue.
    Gentler titles let us use,
    Hate each other, but not abuse.   85
JOAN. Pretty dear!
PUNCH. Ah! ma chère!
BOTH. Joy of my life and only care.

Dance and exeunt.

LUCKLESS.

Gentlemen, the next is Charon and a poet. They are disputing about an affair pretty common with poets—going 90
off without paying.

Enter Charon *and a* Poet.

CHARON.

Never tell me, sir, I expect my fare. I wonder what trade
these authors drive in the other world. I would with as good
a will see a soldier aboard my boat. A tattered redcoat and
a tattered black one have bilked me so often that I am re- 95
solved never to take either of them up again unless I am paid
beforehand.

POET.

What a wretched thing it is to be poor. My body lay a fortnight in the other world before it was buried. And this
fellow has kept my spirit a month, sunning himself on the 100
other side of the river, because my pockets were empty. Wilt
thou be so kind as to show me the way to the Court of
Nonsense?

CHARON.

Ha, ha, ha! The Court of Nonsense! Why pray, sir, what
have you to do there? These rags look more like the dress of 105
one of Apollo's people than of Nonsense's.

POET.

Why fellow, didst thou never carry rags to Nonsense?

CHARON.

Truly sir, I cannot say but I have, but it is a long time ago,
I assure you. If you are really bound thither, I'll set your

name down in my pocketbook, and I don't question your 110
honor's payment. Nonsense is the best deity to me in the
shades. Look at that account, sir.

POET (*reads*).

Spirits imported for the Goddess of Nonsense since October,
in the year ——: five people of great quality, seven ordinary
courtiers, nineteen attorneys, eleven counselors, twenty-six 115
justices of the peace, and one hundred Presbyterian parsons.
—These courtiers and people of quality pay swingingly, I
suppose?

CHARON.

Not always. I have wafted over many a spirit in a laced coat
who has been forced to leave it with me.   120

LUCKLESS.

Gentlemen, the next is one of Charon's men with a prisoner.

Enter Sailor *and a* Sexton.

CHARON.

How now?

SAILOR.

We have caught the rogue at last. This is Mr. Robgrave the
sexton who has plundered so many spirits.

CHARON.

Are you come at last, sir? What have you to say for yourself? 125
Ha, what's become of all the jewels and other valuable things
you have stolen? Where are they, sirrah? Ha!

SEXTON.

Alackaday, I am an unfortunate poor rogue. The church-
wardens and clerks have had them all; I had only a small
reward for stealing them.   130

CHARON.

Then you shall have another reward here, sir. Carry him
before Justice Minos immediately. Away with him.

Exeunt Sailor *and* Sexton.

---

113. *Spirits . . . Nonsense*] Charon's itemized account may have been
suggested by Jean-François Regnard's *La descente de Mazzetin aux enfers*
(1689). This play was printed in *Le Théatre Italien de Gherardi* (Amsterdam:
Braakman, 1701), which Fielding certainly knew. It would be fair to say
that Regnard developed hints from Lucian, and Fielding—a life-long
admirer of Lucian—was probably indebted to both.

POET.

> Who knows whether this rogue has not robbed me too. I
> forgot to look in upon my body before I came away.

CHARON.

> Had you anything of value buried with you?   135

POET.

> Things of inestimable value—six folios of my own works.

LUCKLESS.

> Most poets of this age will have their works buried with them.

Enter Sailor.

SAILOR.

> There is a great number of passengers arrived from Eng-
> land, all bound to the Court of Nonsense.

CHARON.

> Some plague, I suppose, or a fresh cargo of physicians come 140
> to town from the universities. Or perhaps a war broke out.

SAILOR.

> No, no, these are all authors, and a war never sends any of
> them hither.

LUCKLESS.

> Now, gentlemen, I shall produce such a set of figures as I
> may defy all Europe except our own playhouses to equal. 145
> Come, put away.

Enter Don Tragedio, Sir Farcical Comic, Dr. Orator, Signior Opera,
Monsieur Pantomime, *and* Mrs. Novel.

146.1–2] Although the Sailor has just announced this group as authors,
they are types of entertainment and would, some far more definitely than
others, be associated with living persons, as explained in Appendix B.
They are: Don Tragedio, *Lewis Theobald*; Sir Farcical Comick, *Colley
Cibber*; Dr. Orator, *John Henley*; Signior Opera, *Francesco Senesino*; Monsieur
Pantomime, *John Rich*; Mrs. Novel, *Eliza Haywood*.

146.1. *Don Tragedio*] The Don's Spanish title comes in part from the
high-flown honor themes associated with Spain, but it is worthy of note
that three new tragedies of the 1729–1730 season had Spanish characters
and a Spanish setting: *The Rape*, an anonymous reworking of Nicholas
Brady's tragedy of 1692 (L.I.F., Nov. 25, 1729); Osborne Sidney Wandes-
ford, *Fatal Love* (H., Jan. 21, 1730); Thomas Walker, *The Fate of Villainy*
(G.F., Feb. 24, 1730). None could be called a success, and the second of
them was said by its author to have failed because of the ineptness of the
performers—many of whom were to appear two months later in *The
Author's Farce*.

POET.

>Ha! Don Tragedio, your most obedient servant. Sir Farcical,
>Dr. Orator, I am heartily glad to see you. Dear Signior
>Opera. Monsieur Pantomime. Mrs. Novel in the shades
>too! What lucky distemper can have sent so much good 150
>company hither?

TRAGEDIO.

>A tragedy occasioned me to die,
>That perishing the first day, so did I.

FARCICAL.

>An entertainment sent me out of the world. My life went out
>in a hiss. Stap my breath! 155

AIR IV, Silvia, My Dearest

OPERA.

>Claps universal,
>Applauses resounding,
>Hisses confounding
>Attending my song.
>My senses drowned 160
>And I fell down dead,
>Whilst I was singing, ding, dang, dong.

POET.

>Well, Monsieur Pantomime, how came you by your fate?

PANTOMIME (*makes signs to his neck*).

POET.

>Broke his neck. Alas, poor gentleman. And you, Madam
>Novel? 165

NOVEL.

>Mine was a hard case indeed.

---

154. *An entertainment*] The hissing of Cibber's pastoral entertainment, *Love in a Riddle*, was also noted in II.i.

155. *Stap my breath!*] As comic actor, Cibber was best known for his foppish roles; in a sense, three of his most famous fops were the same character. Sir Novelty Fashion in his own *Love's Last Shift* (1696), whose favorite phrase is "Stop my vitals," was raised to the peerage by Vanbrugh in *The Relapse* (1696) as Lord Foppington; the elevation in rank flattened his lordship's vowels, so that he now exclaims "Stap my vitals!" "Stap my breath" is said only by Lord Foppington in Cibber's *The Careless Husband* (1704), the third and least interesting portrayal of this prince of coxcombs.

AIR V, *'Twas When the Seas Were Roaring*

   Oh! Pity all a maiden
     Condemned hard fates to prove;
   I rather would have laid in
     Than thus have died for love.   170
   'Twas hard t'encounter death-a
     Before the bridal bed.
   Ah! Would I had kept my breath-a
     And lost my maidenhead.

POET.

   Poor lady!   175

LUCKLESS.

   'Twas a hard fate indeed, in this age.

CHARON.

   Well, my masters, I wish you well. I must take leave of you.
   If you follow that path you'll arrive at the Court of Nonsense.

                              Exit Charon.

POET.

   Gentlemen, if you please I'll show you the way.   *Exeunt.*

LUCKLESS.

   The next, gentlemen, is a blackamoor lady who comes to 180
   present you with a saraband and castanets.   *A dance.*

LUCKLESS.

   Now, gentlemen and ladies, I shall produce a bookseller who
   is the Prime Minister of Nonsense, and the Poet.

              Enter Bookseller *and* Poet.

POET.

   'Tis strange, 'tis wondrous strange!

BOOKSELLER.

   And yet 'tis true. Did you observe her eyes?   185

183.] Since Dr. Orator alone of these six does not explain how he came
to die, possibly a line has dropped out and that given to him at this point
in O4 ("A Muggletonian Dog stabb'd me.") is part of the original text.

184. *'tis wondrous strange!*] *Hamlet*, I.ii.220, or *Othello*, I.iii.160, might
have suggested this tragic diction; or perhaps Lee's *Theodosius*, I.i.79,
89–90:

       'Tis strange! O Athenais! wondrous . . .
             If it be true,
     I say again, by Heav'n 'tis wond'rous strange.

POET.

Her ears rather, for there she took the infection. She saw the Signior's visage in his voice.

BOOKSELLER.

Did you not mark how she melted when he sung?

POET.

I saw her like another Dido. I saw her heart rise up to her eyes, and drop down again to her ears.   190

BOOKSELLER.

That a woman of so much sense as the Goddess of Nonsense should be taken thus at first sight! I have served her faithfully these thirty years as a bookseller in the upper world, and never knew her guilty of one folly before.

POET.

Nay certainly, Mr. Curry, you know as much of her as any 195 man.

BOOKSELLER.

I think I ought. I am sure I have made as large oblations to her as all Warwick Lane and Paternoster Row.

POET.

But is she this night to be married to Signior Opera?

BOOKSELLER.

This is to be the bridal night. Well, this will be the strangest 200 thing that has happened in the shades since the rape of Proserpine. But now I think on't, what news bring you from the other world?

POET.

Why, affairs go much in the same road there as when you were alive: authors starve and booksellers grow fat, Grub 205 Street harbors as many pirates as ever Algiers did, they have more theaters than are at Paris, and just as much wit as there is at Amsterdam, they have ransacked all Italy for singers and all France for dancers.

---

195. *Mr. Curry*] The name of course suggests Edmund Curll; see Appendix B.

198. *Warwick . . . Row*] The booksellers who had their shows in these streets near St. Paul's seem to have done a thriving business in pamphlets and other inexpensive publications.

201–202. *rape of Proserpine*] One of the most popular of recent pantomimes was Lewis Theobald's *The Rape of Proserpine* (L.I.F., Feb. 13, 1727).

BOOKSELLER.

And all hell for conjurers.   210

POET.

My Lord Mayor has shortened the time of Bartholomew
Fair in Smithfield, and so they are resolved to keep it all the
year round at the other end of the town.

BOOKSELLER.

I find matters go swimmingly. But I fancy I am wanted. If
you please, sir, I will show you the way.   215

POET.

Sir, I follow you.   *Exeunt.*

Enter Joan, Lady Kingcall, Mrs. Glassring, *and* Mrs. Cheat'em.

JOAN.

I ask leave.

ALL.

With you, madam.

JOAN.

Clubs, and the king of hearts.

GLASSRING.

Sure never was anything so provoking as this; you always 220
put me out of a great game.   *They play.*

---

210. *all . . . conjurers*] a thrust at pantomimes like *The Necromancer, or
Harlequin Doctor Faustus* (L.I.F., Dec. 20, 1723) and Lewis Theobald's
Harlequin, a Sorcerer, with the Loves of Pluto and Proserpine (L.I.F., Feb. 21,
1725).

211. *shortened . . . Fair*] In 1717 Bartholomew Fair was limited to three
days instead of two weeks owing "to the Great Vice and Profaness, occasion'd
there by Stage-Plays." In 1730, however, dramatic performances at the
booths seem to have continued for a fortnight.

217–226. *I ask . . . diamond*] The game of ombre in Pope's *Rape of the
Lock* may have suggested staging a game of quadrille, a four-handed
French variation of ombre that had been played in England for four or
five years. Most of the rules of ombre apply; there is no stock, however, as
the entire pack of forty cards (eights, nines, and tens are not used) is dealt
out, each player receiving ten. Instead of one player always opposing the
others, the "ombre" in quadrille may have a partner. If the player whose
privilege it is to bid doubts whether he can take more tricks than the other
three players but nevertheless feels that he and a partner with at least one
strong card may well have six tricks, he "asks leave" to "call for a king."
This permission is granted if each of the other players also lacks faith in his

KINGCALL.

There's your king, madam; you have called very luckily this time. Spadille. There's basto. We have won our game.

JOAN.

I say nothing.

KINGCALL.

I'll play it. 225

GLASSRING.

Then you have lost it: there is the best diamond.

JOAN.

Was ever such play seen? I would not play with Lady Kingcall for farthings.

KINGCALL.

I have seen your ladyship make greater mistakes.

JOAN.

I wish you'd name when, madam. 230

KINGCALL.

I have not so good a memory, madam.

JOAN.

I am sorry for it, madam, for you seem to want one. It might be of use to you.

KINGCALL.

I wish you had a better, madam. It might be of use to others. 235

JOAN.

What do you mean, madam?

KINGCALL.

I mean that you owe me a guinea.

---

unaided hand. The bidder then names trumps and calls for a king of another suit; the player who holds the called-for king becomes his "friend" or partner. Joan and Lady Kingcall are partners who take the first six tricks ("We have won our game"), the latter winning the last three with the king of Hearts, the ace of spades (spadille, the highest trump regardless of suit), and the ace of clubs (basto, the third-highest trump regardless of suit). Thereupon the partners have the option of trying to make a vole (or slam), and Lady Kingcall ventures ("I'll play it"); the reason for Joan's "I say nothing" is that the rules forbade encouraging or discouraging a "friend" who is in the position to take this step. Lady Kingcall suffers a lapse of memory and plays a diamond which Mrs. Glassring is able to top; the loss of a single trick defeats the attempt for a vole, so that Joan and Lady Kingcall fail to win the high stakes that seemed within their grasp.

JOAN.

I believe, madam, you forget you owe me two.

KINGCALL.

Madam, I deny it.

JOAN.

And I deny yours.   240

GLASSRING, CHEAT'EM.

Oh fie, ladies!

KINGCALL.

It's happy for your enemies that your ladyship's character is
so well known.

JOAN.

It would become anybody to say so, better than you. I
never stole china.   245

KINGCALL.

You are an impudent sow.

JOAN.

You are an old, ugly sow, and I'll make you know it.

They fight.

Enter Punch.

PUNCH.

Have I caught you, madam? I'll put an end to your
quadrille, I am resolved. Get you home, strumpet. And
you are the fine ladies who bring her to this. I'll drive all 250
of you.

Kicks them out and overturns the table.

LUCKLESS.

Very uncivilly done, truly, Master Punch.

PUNCH.

Uncivilly! Why, sir, since this game of quadrille has been
in fashion she has never looked after my family; she does
nothing but eat, drink, sleep, dress, and play at quadrille. 255

AIR VI, *To You Fair Ladies*

To all you husbands and you wives
    This Punchinello sings,
For reformation of your lives
    This good advice he brings:
That if you would avoid all ill,   260
You should leave off the dear quadrille.

> No tyrant on earth his slaves
>   With greater terror awes,
> With force more absolute behaves,
>   Nor gives severer laws.   265
> Unequal though his taxes fall,
> They're with a smile received by all.

> How many beauties rich in charms
>   Are subject to his will.
> The bride when in the bridegroom's arms   270
>   Still thinks on dear quadrille.
> Her spouse her body may enroll,
> Quadrille is master of her soul.

> The China people (sailors say)
>   When they have lost their pence   275
> Their family and selves will play;
>   Heaven keep that custom hence!
> For beauties of the first degree
> May so be slaves to some marquis.   *Exit* Punch.

LUCKLESS.

Gentlemen, the next figures are Somebody and Nobody, 280
who come to present you with a dance.

Enter Somebody *and* Nobody. *They dance.*

---

280. *Somebody and Nobody*] The Nobody theme started in Germany in
the sixteenth century with the idea "Nobody is responsible for the disorder
in a household." The pun worked differently in different languages; in
English illustrations it led to a figure with almost no body, the legs coming
up almost to the neck. Nobody was soon joined by Somebody, with a very
prominent trunk. The pair have a theatrical history in England going
back at least to 1606 when the play entitled *No-body, and Somebody* was
printed for John Trundle "at the signe of No-body." In the early eighteenth
century the pair occasionally appeared on the human stage, but representation by puppets was probably more common: it would have been easy to
construct and costume puppets that would look like the figures drawn by
graphic satirists, e.g., Hogarth in 1732. One puppet performance, a
"pacifick dance between Somebody and Nobody," offered as part of an
entertainment by Madame de la Nash on May 20, 1748, is worth mention-
ing, since Madame de la Nash was simply a cover name for an enterprise of
Fielding's.

AIR VII, *Black Joke*

SOMEBODY.	Of all the men in London town,
	Or knaves or fools, in coat or gown,
	The representative am I.
NOBODY.	Go through the world and you will find 285
	In all the classes of humankind
	Many a jolly Nobody.

                For him a Nobody sure we may call
                Who during his life does nothing at all
                        But eat and snore   290
                        And drink and roar,
        From whore to the tavern, from tavern to whore,
                With a laced coat, and that is all.   [*Exeunt.*]

LUCKLESS.

Gentlemen, this is the end of the first interlude.

[*The curtain closes.*]

LUCKLESS.

Now, gentlemen, I shall present you with the most glorious 295
scene that has ever appeared on the stage. It is the Court of
Nonsense. Play away, soft music, and draw up the curtain.

The curtain drawn up to soft music, discovers the Goddess of Nonsense *on a
throne, the* Orator *in a Tub,* Tragedio, *etc. attending.*

NONSENSE.

    Let all my votaries prepare
    To celebrate this joyful day.

294.] The curtain must have been closed here if not earlier during the
puppet show. Probably Luckless leaves the stage for a short time, as he
would at the end of an act, though all early texts have only a printer's
ornament separating this speech from his next.

295–296. *most glorious scene*] Fielding is following closely the staging of the
transition between Acts IV and V in Buckingham's *The Rehearsal*, where
Act V begins with Bayes returning after the *entr'acte* interval announcing,
"Now, Gentlemen, I'l shew you the greatest Scene that England ever saw,"
followed by a stage direction showing that the curtain opened on a striking
tableau.

297.2. *Orator in a tub*] "The pulpit of a Dissenter is usually called a Tub;
but that of Mr. Orator *Henley* was covered with velvet, and adorned with
gold" (Scriblerus' note on "Henley's gilt Tub," *Dunciad*, II, 2).

LUCKLESS.

Gentlemen, observe what a lover of recitativo Nonsense is. 300

NONSENSE.

Monsieur Pantomime, you are welcome.

PANTOMIME (*cuts a caper*).

NONSENSE.

Alas, poor gentleman! He is modest. You may speak: no
words offend that have no wit in them.

LUCKLESS.

Why, Madam Nonsense, don't you know that Monsieur
Pantomime is dumb? And yet let me tell you, he has been of 305
great service to you: he is the only one of your votaries that
sets people asleep without talking. But here's Don Tragedio
will make noise enough.

TRAGEDIO.

Yes, Tragedio is indeed my name,

Long since recorded in the rolls of fame   }   310

At Lincoln's Inn and eke at Drury Lane.

Let everlasting thunder sound my praise

And forked lightning in my scutcheon blaze.

To Shakespeare, Jonson, Dryden, Lee, or Rowe

I not a line, no, not a thought do owe.   315

Me, for my novelty, let all adore,

For as I wrote none ever wrote before.

NONSENSE.

Thou art doubly welcome, welcome.

TRAGEDIO.

That welcome, yes, that welcome is my due.

Two tragedies I wrote, and wrote for you.   320

And had not hisses, hisses me dismayed,

By this, I'd writ two score, two score, by jay'd.

LUCKLESS.

By jay'd! Aye, that's another excellence of the Don's; he
does not only glean up all the bad words of other authors but
makes new bad words of his own.   325

---

322. *by jay'd*] If this is anything more than a meaningless coinage
ridiculing archaisms proposed by Theobald in his efforts to "restore"
Shakespeare, its significance has escaped me.

FARCICAL.

Nay, egad, I have made new words, and spoiled old ones too, if you talk of that. I have made foreigners break English and Englishmen break Latin. I have as great a confusion of languages in my play as was at the building of Babel.

LUCKLESS.

And so much the more extraordinary because the author 330 understands no language at all.

FARCICAL.

No language at all! Stap my vitals!

LUCKLESS.

But Sir Farcical, I hear you had once an intention to introduce a set of marrowbones and cleavers upon the stage.

FARCICAL.

'Tis true. And I did produce one bone, but it stuck so 335 confoundedly in the stomach of the audience that I was obliged to drop the project.

NONSENSE.

Dr. Orator, I have heard of you.

---

326. *made . . . ones*] Cibber's misuse of language had been attacked for years, but there had been nothing to equal the ridicule which greeted his Preface to *The Provoked Husband* (1728); chapter XVI of *Peri Bathous* is the best-known response, but the charge here that "the author understands no language at all," the immediately following reference to "one bone," and the hilarious misspelling *paraphonalia* (l. 671 below) shows that such jokes were still current two years later.

332. *Stap my vitals!*] See note to line 155 above.

335. *I . . . bone*] The story begins with the stormy first performance of *The Provoked Husband* on Jan. 10, 1728. An audience ready to damn Cibber knew that the play was partly his, partly work left unfinished by Vanbrugh. The play had a "genteel" plot and a "low" plot; misled by the prologue, they assumed that the low plot was mainly Cibber's. This led to a nearly fatal interruption in Act IV when the landlady responded to her guest's complaint of hunger with, "Good lack! here's Company, Sir; will you give me leave to get you a broil'd Bone, or so, till the Ladies come home, Sir?" The reaction of the audience was one that, an eyewitness reports, "I thought it impossible to outlive." The journals played merrily with Cibber's bone, even after Cibber's publication of the incomplete draft, which showed that the offending bone was Vanbrugh's.

338. *Dr. . . . you*] In his *Oratory Transactions, No. II* (*c.* 1729) Henley had published "A Dissertation on *Nonsense*"; even without this, the Goddess would have heard of him.

ORATOR.

Aye, and you might have heard me too; I bawled loud
enough, I'm sure.   340

LUCKLESS.

She might have heard you. But if she had understood your
advertisements I will believe Nonsense to have more understanding that Apollo.

ORATOR.

Have understood me, sir! What has understanding to do?
My hearers would be diverted, and they are so, which could 345
not be if understanding were necessary, because very few of
them have any.

NONSENSE.

You've all deserved my hearty thanks— (*to* Signior Opera)
but here my treasure I bestow.

AIR VIII, *Lillibolera*

OPERA.   Let the foolish philosopher strive in his cell,   350
  By wisdom or virtue to merit true praise,
The soldier in hardship and danger still dwell
  That glory and honor may crown his last days,
   The patriot sweat
   To be thought great,   355
Or beauty all day at the looking glass toil,
   That popular voices
   May ring their applauses,
While a breath is the only reward of their coil.

But would you a wise man to action incite,   360
  Be riches proposed the reward of his pain,
In riches is centered all human delight,
  No joy is on earth but what gold can obtain.
   If women, wine,
   Or grandeur fine   365
Be most your delight, all these riches can.
   Would you have men to flatter?
   To be rich is the matter;
When you cry, he is rich, you cry a great man.

---

350. *Lillibolera*] Lilli Burleo, lillibullero, lilibolaro are among the recorded spellings of this most popular tune; the final *a* appears in O1–4,
but may be a misprint.

NONSENSE (*repeating in an ecstasy*).

    "When you cry, he is rich, you cry a great man."   370
    Bravissimo! I long to be your wife.

NOVEL.

    If all my romances ever pleased the ear of my goddess, if
    I ever found favor in her sight—oh, do not rob me thus!

NONSENSE.

    What means my daughter?

NOVEL.

    Alas, he is my husband.   375

BOOKSELLER.

    But though he were your husband in the other world, death
    solves that tie, and he is at liberty now to take another.
    And I never knew any one instance of a husband here who
    would take the same wife again.

AIR IX, *Whilst I Gaze on Cloe Trembling*

NOVEL.   May all maids from me take warning   380
                How a lover's arms they fly;
        Lest the first kind offer scorning,
                They, without a second, die.

        How unhappy is my passion!
                How tormenting is my pain!   385
        If you thwart my inclination,
                Let me die for love again.

BOOKSELLER.

    Again! What, did you die for love of your husband?

NOVEL.

    He knows he ought to have been so. He swore he would be
    so. Yes, he knows I died for love, for I died in childbed.   390

ORATOR.

    Why, madam, did you not tell me all the road hither that
    you was a virgin?

---

370. *When . . . rich*] This line ecstatically repeated by Nonsense may have
overtones. In all early texts it is given: "*When you cry he is Rich, you cry a
Great Man.*" Capitalizing adjectives is not usual. The phrase "great man"
would at this time be applied to Walpole if context gave even a remote
handle (as it did for Punch in the revised version of the play; see below,
p. 98); but in this generally non-political play the point is hard to see.
Nor does the other adjective point easily to John Rich (who is at the
moment on stage as Monsieur Pantomime).

AIR X, *Highland Laddy*

[OPERA.]
> I was told in my life
>> Death forever
>> Did dissever   395
> Men from every mortal strife,
> And that greatest plague, a wife.

> For had the priests possessed men
>> That to Tartarus
>> Wives came after us,   400
> Their devil would be a jest then,
> And our devil a wife.

NONSENSE.

> Avaunt, polluted wretch, begone!
> Think not I'll take pollution to my arms.
> No, no—no, no—no, no, no.   405

OPERA.

Well, since I can't have a goddess, I'll e'en prove a man of honor. I was always in love with thee, my angel.

NOVEL.

Now I am happy, verily.

OPERA.

My long-lost dear!

NOVEL.

My new-found bud!   410

AIR XI, *Dusty Miller*

[OPERA].
> Will my charming creature
>> Once again receive me?
> Though I proved a traitor
>> Will she still believe me?

---

393. S.P.] Since O1–3 give no speech heading it at first might appear that the song belongs to Dr. Orator. Yet (especially in view of further dropped speech headings in Airs XI and XX in O1–3) we may conclude that the reading of O4 is correct and the song belongs to Signior Opera; otherwise Nonsense's response is dramatically awkward and the fine reversal between Airs X and XI is lost.

411. S.P.] Again a dropped speech prefix, but here there is no possible doubt that the song is begun by Signior Opera. O4 so heads it, and may retain the original idea also in heading the last four lines of the song "*Both.*"

I will well repay thee   415
  For past faults of roving,
Nor shall any day be
  Without proofs of loving.

On that tender lilly breast
  Whilest I lie panting,   420
Both together blest,
  Both with transports fainting.
Sure no human hearts
  Were ever so delighted.
Death, which others parts,   425
  Hath our souls united.

AIR XII, *Over the Hills and Far Away*

OPERA. Were I laid on Scotland's coast,
  And in my arms embraced my dear,
Let scrubado do its most,
  I would know no grief or fear.   430

NOVEL. Were we cast on Ireland's soil,
  There confined in bogs to dwell,
For thee potatoes I would boil,
  No Irish spouse should feast so well.

OPERA. And though we scrubbed it all the day,   435
NOVEL. We'd kiss and hug the night away.
OPERA. Scotch and Irish both should say,
BOTH.   Oh, how blest, how blest are they!
ORATOR.

Since my Goddess is disengaged from one lover, may the
humblest, yet not the least diligent of her servants, hope she 440
would smile on him?

LUCKLESS.

Master Orator, you had best try to charm the Goddess with
an oration.

ORATOR.

The history of a fiddle and a fiddlestick is going to be held
forth.   445

---

427. *Were . . . coast*] A parody (to the same tune) of the duet in Act I of
The Beggar's Opera, "Were I laid on Greenland's coast."
 429. *scrubado*] the itch.

A fiddle is a statesman: why? because it's hollow. A fiddlestick is a drunkard: why? because it loves rosening.

LUCKLESS.

Gentlemen, observe how he balances his hands: his left
hand is the fiddle and his right hand is the fiddlestick.

ORATOR.

A fiddle is like a beau's nose because the bridge is often 450
down; a fiddlestick is like a mountebank because it plays
upon a crowd. A fiddle is like a stockjobber's tongue because
it sounds different notes; and a fiddlestick is like a stockjobber's wig because it has a great deal of horsehair in it.

LUCKLESS.

And your oration is like yourself because it has a great deal 455
of nonsense in it.

NONSENSE.

In vain you try to charm my ears unless by music.

ORATOR.

Have at you then.

LUCKLESS.

Gentlemen, observe how the Doctor sings in his tub. Here
are no wires, all alive, alive, ho!   460

ORATOR.

Chimes of the Times, to the tune of Moll Pately.

AIR XIII, *Moll Pately*

All men are birds by nature, sir,
   Though they have not wings to fly;
On earth a soldier's a creature, sir,
   Much resembling a kite in the sky;   465

---

446. *rosening*] rubbing with rosin, and (dialectal) indulging in drink.
450. *like . . . nose*] the old joke about syphilis attacking the nasal septum.
451–452. *plays . . . crowd*] a pun upon the dialectal sense of crowd as
fiddle.
461. *Chimes of the Times*] Apparently Henley either sang or chanted part
of his performance, and in 1728 he began to advertise the "Chimes of the
Times" as a regular feature of his programs.
462. *All . . . birds*] Henley was fond of comparing men to other members
of the animal kingdom. One hearer reported: "He proved very learnedly
and metaphysically that every Thing was *Fish*, and that the World was
nothing but a great *Fish-Pond*, where Mankind laid Baits to ensnare and
catch one another."

The physician is a fowl, sir,
Whom most men call an owl, sir,
    Who by his hooting,
    Hooting, hooting,
    Hooting, hooting,   470
    Hooting, hooting,
Tells us that death is nigh.

The usurer is a swallow, sir,
    That can swallow gold by the jorum;
A woodcock is Squire Shallow, sir;   475
    And a goose is oft of the quorum;
    The gamester is a rook, sir;
    The lawyer, with his Coke, sir,
        Is but a raven
        Croaking, croaking,   480
        Croaking, croaking,
        Croaking, croaking
After the ready rhinorum.

Young virgins are scarce as rails, sir;
    Plenty as bats the nightwalkers go;   485
Soft Italians are nightingales, sir,
    And a cock sparrow mimics a beau.
    Like birds men are to be caught, sir,
    Like birds men are to be bought, sir.
        Men of a side   490
        Like birds of a feather
        Will flock together,
        Will flock together,
Both sexes like birds will———too.

NONSENSE.

'Tis all in vain.   495

TRAGEDIO.

Is Nonsense of me then forgetful grown,
And must the Signior be preferred alone?

---

474. *jorum*] a large drinking bowl.
478. *Coke*] Sir Edward Coke (1552–1634), the great authority on the
English common law.
483. *the ready rhinorum*] an elaboration of "the ready Rhino," a slang
expression for money.

Is it for this, for this, ye gods, that I
Have in one scene made some folks laugh, some cry?
For this does my low blustering language creep,   500
At once to wake you and to make you sleep?

FARCICAL.

And so all my puns and quibbles and conundrums are
quite forgotten, stap my vitals! But surely Your Goddessship
will remember a certain thing called a pastoral.

ORATOR.

More Chimes of the Times, to the tune of Rogues, Rogues, 505
Rogues.

AIR XIV, *There Was a Jovial Beggar*

The stone that all things turns at will
        To gold, the chemist craves;
But gold, without the chemist's skill,
        Turns all men into knaves.   510
                For a-cheating they will go, etc.

The merchant would the courtier cheat
        When on his goods he lays
Too high a price, but faith he's bit,
        For a courtier never pays.   515
                For a-cheating they will go, etc.

The lawyer, with a face demure,
        Hangs him who steals your pelf,
Because the good man can endure
        No robber but himself.   520
                For a-cheating, etc.

Betwixt the quack and highwayman
        What difference can there be?
Though this with pistol, that with pen,
        Both kill you for a fee.   525
                For a-cheating, etc.

The husband cheats his loving wife,
        And to a mistress goes,
While she at home, to ease her life,
        Carouses with the beaus.   530
                For a-cheating, etc.

---

504. *a pastoral*] another reference to Cibber's *Love in a Riddle*.

The tenant doth the steward nick
 (So low this art we find),
The steward doth his lordship trick,
 My lord tricks all mankind.   535
   For a-cheating, etc.

One sect there are to whose fair lot
 No cheating arts do fall,
And those are parsons called, God wot:
 And so I cheat you all.   540
   For a-cheating, etc.

    Enter Charon.

CHARON.

 An't please Your Majesty, there is an odd sort of a man o'
t'other side the water, says he's recommended to you by
some people of quality. Egad, I don't care to take him
aboard, not I. He says his name is Hurloborumbo—rumbo 545
—Hurloborumbolo, I think he calls himself. He looks like
one of Apollo's people in my opinion; he seems to me mad
enough to be a real poet.

NONSENSE.

 Take him aboard.

CHARON.

 I had forgot to tell your ladyship, I hear rare news; they 550
say you are to be declared Goddess of Wit.

BOOKSELLER.

 That's no news, Mr. Charon.

CHARON.

 Well, I'll take Hurloborumbo aboard.   *Exit* Charon.

ORATOR.

 I must win the Goddess before he arrives, or else I shall
lose her forever. —A Rap at the Times.   555

   AIR XV, *When I Was a Dame of Honor*

 Come all who've heard my cushion beat,
  Confess me as full of dullness
 As any egg is full of meat
  Or full moon is of fullness.

---

 545. *Hurloborumbo*] again Johnson of Cheshire's *Hurlothrumbo*, already
mentioned by Witmore in I.v.

Let the justice and his clerk both own 560
    Than theirs my dullness greater,
And tell how I've harangued the town
    When I was a bold orator.

The lawyer wrangling at the bar
    While the reverend bench is dozing, 565
The scribbler in a pamphlet war,
    Or Grub Street bard composing,
The trudging quack in scarlet cloak
    Or coffeehouse politic prater,
Can none come up to what I have spoke 570
    When I was a bold orator.

The well-bred courtier telling lies
    Or levee hunter believing,
The vain coquette that rolls her eyes,
    More empty fops deceiving, 575
The parson of dissenting gang
    Or flattering dedicator,
Could none of them like me harangue
    When I was a bold orator.

Enter Punch.

PUNCH.

You, you, you. 580

LUCKLESS.

What's the matter, Punch?

PUNCH.

Who is that?

LUCKLESS.

That's an orator, master Punch.

PUNCH.

An orator, what's that?

LUCKLESS.

Why, an orator is—is—egad, I can't tell what; he is a 585
man that nobody dares dispute with.

PUNCH.

Say you so, I'll be with him presently. Bring out my tub

there. I'll dispute with you, I'll warrant. I am a Muggletonian.

ORATOR.

    I am not. 590

PUNCH.

    Then you are not of my opinion.

ORATOR.

    Sirrah, I know that you and your whole tribe would be the
death of me, but I am resolved to proceed to confute you as
I have done hitherto, and as long as I have breath you shall
hear me, and I hope I have breath enough to blow you all 595
out of the world.

PUNCH.

    If noise will.

ORATOR.

    Sir, I—

PUNCH.

    Hear me, sir.

NONSENSE.

    Hear him, hear him, hear him. 600

AIR XVI, *Hey Barnaby, Take it for Warning*

PUNCH.   No tricks shall save your bacon,
          Orator, Orator, you are mistaken,
          Punch will not be thus confuted.
          Bring forth your reasons or you are nonsuited.
               Heigh ho. 605
          No tricks shall save your bacon,
          Orator, Orator, you are mistaken.

ORATOR.   Instead of reasons advancing,
          Let the dispute be concluded by dancing.
               Ti, to.   *They dance.* 610

NONSENSE.

    'Tis all in vain. A virgin I will live. And oh great Signior,
prithee take this chaplet and still wear it for my sake.

588–589. *Muggletonian*] The radical religious ideas of Lodowick Muggleton
(1609–1698) still had adherents among the lower classes; Henley's manu-
scripts included four volumes of lectures against the Muggletonians in
1728 and 1729.

TRAGEDIO.

    And does great Nonsense then at length determine
    To give the chaplet to that singing vermin?

NONSENSE.

    I do.   615

TRAGEDIO.

    Then Opera come on, and let us try
    Whether shall wear the chaplet, you or I.

AIR XVII, *Be Kind and Love*

NOVEL.   Oh, spare to take his precious life away;
             So sweet a voice must sure your passion lay.
             Oh hear his gentle murmurs first, and then   620
             If you can kill him, I will cry amen.

TRAGEDIO.

    Since but a song you ask, a song I'll hear.
    But tell him that last song is his last prayer.

AIR XVIII

OPERA.   Barbarous cruel man,
    I'll sing thus while I'm dying, I'm dying like a swan,   625
        I'm dying like a swan,
           A swan,
           A swan,
    With my face all pale and wan.
    More fierce art thou than pirates,   630
        Than pirates,
    Whom the sirens' music charms,
        Alarms,
        Disarms.
    More fierce than men on the high roads,   635
        On the high - - - - - roads,
        On the high - - - - - roads,
    More fierce than men on the high roads
    Whom Polly Peachum warms.
        The devil   640
        Was made civil

---

624. *Barbarous cruel man*] Sung by Stoppelaer, this was the most popular song from the play. The music has not been recovered and no air is named; it was certainly specially composed, possibly by Seedo.

    639. *Polly Peachum*] the heroine of *The Beggar's Opera*.

By Orpheus' tuneful charms.
   And ca - - - - -
       - - - - - - - n
He gentler prove than man? 645

TRAGEDIO.

I cannot do it! *Sheathes his sword.*
Methinks I feel my flesh congealed to bone,
And know not when I'm flesh and blood, or stone.

PANTOMIME (*runs several times round the stage*).

NONSENSE.

Alas, what means Monsieur Pantomime?

BOOKSELLER.

By his pointing to his head, I suppose he would have the 650
chaplet.

NONSENSE.

Pretty youth!

NOVEL.

Oh, my dear, how shall I express the trouble of my soul?

OPERA.

If there be sympathy in love, I'm sure I felt it, for I was in a
damnable fright too. 655

NOVEL.

Give me a buss, then.

AIR XIX, *Under the Greenwood Tree*

In vain a thousand heroes and kings
   Should court me to their arms,
In vain should give me a thousand fine things,
   For thee I'd reserve my charms. 660
On that dear breast, entranced in joys,
   Oh, let me ever be.
OPERA.   Oh, how I will kiss thee,
How I'll embliss thee,
When thou art abed with me. 665

---

647. *Methinks ... bone*] Many tragedies of the time would furnish
parallels to this couplet, but one from Theobald's *The Persian Princess*
(IV.ii) will suffice:

   Speak in the Name of Horror, all thy Tydings;
   Tho' they have force to freeze my youthful Blood,
   And turn me to a Statue with Confusion.

NONSENSE (*repeats*).

> Oh, how I will kiss thee, etc.

FARCICAL.

> Since nothing but a song will do, I will have my song too.

LUCKLESS.

> Gentlemen, pray observe and take notice how Sir Farcical's
> song sets Nonsense asleep.

AIR XX, *Hunt the Squirrel*

[FARCICAL.]
> Can my Goddess then forget   670
> Paraphonalia,
> Paraphonalia?
> Can she the crown on another head set
> Than of her Paraphonalia?
> If that had not done too,   675
> Remember my bone too,
> My bone, my bone, my bone.
> Sure my Goddess never can
> Forget my marrowbone.

BOOKSELLER.

> Nonsense is asleep.   680

TRAGEDIO.

> Oh, ye immortal powers!

FARCICAL.

> If anything can wake her, 'tis a dance.

OMNES.

> A dance, a dance, a dance!

Enter Charon.

LUCKLESS.

> How now, Charon? You are not to enter yet.

CHARON.

> To enter sir! Alackaday, we are all undone. Here is a 685
> constable and Mr. Murdertext the Presbyterian parson
> coming in.

---

671. *Paraphonalia*] Cibber's notorious misspelling in the Preface to *The
Provoked Husband*, though corrected in the second edition, remained a jest
for years.

676. *my bone*] See note on l. 335 above.

Enter Murdertext *and* Constable.

CONSTABLE.

Are you the master of the puppet show?

LUCKLESS.

Yes, sir.

CONSTABLE.

Then you must along with me, sir. I have a warrant for 690
you, sir.

LUCKLESS.

For what?

MURDERTEXT.

For abusing Nonsense, sirrah.

CONSTABLE.

People of quality are not to have their diversions libeled at
this rate. 695

MURDERTEXT.

No, sirrah, nor the Saints are not to be abused neither.

LUCKLESS.

Of what do you accuse me, gentlemen?

MURDERTEXT.

Verily I smell a great deal of a—bomination and profaneness. A smell of brimstone offendeth my nostrils, a puppet
show is the devil's house and I will burn it. Shall you abuse 700
Nonsense when the whole town supports it?

LUCKLESS.

Pox on't, had this fellow stayed a few moments longer, till
the dance had been over, I had been easy. Hark you, Mr.
Constable, shall I only beg your patience for one dance, and
then I'll wait on you? 705

MURDERTEXT.

Sirrah, don't try to corrupt the magistrate with thy bribes.
Here shall be no dancing; verily, it is a profane mystery and
hath in it a superfluity of abomination.

NOVEL.

What does this fellow of a constable mean by interrupting
our play? 710

699–700. *a puppet . . . house*] Murdertext's efforts to stop Luckless's show
may owe something to Zeal-of-the-Land Busy's similar attack on Leatherhead's puppets in the last act of Jonson's *Bartholomew Fair*.

AIR XXI, *Fair Dorinda*

Oh Mr. Constable,
    Drunken rascal,
Would I had thee at the Rose.
    Mayst thou be beaten,
    Hanged up and eaten,   715
Mayst thou be eaten, eaten,
      Eaten, eaten,
Eaten by the carrion crows.
The filth that lies in common shores,
    May it ever lie in thy nose,   720
      May it ever
      Lie in thy nose,
Oh, may it lie in thy nose.

LUCKLESS.

Mollify yourself, madam.

MURDERTEXT (*aside*).

Verily that is a pretty creature. It were a piece of charity to 725
take her to myself for a handmaid.

CONSTABLE.

Very pretty, very pretty truly. If magistrates are to be
abused at this rate, the devil may be a constable for me.
Harkee, madam, do you know who we are?

NOVEL.

A rogue, sir.   730

CONSTABLE.

Madam, I'm a constable by day and a justice of peace by
night.

NOVEL.

That is, a buzzard by day and an owl by night.

AIR XXII, *Newmarket*

CONSTABLE.   Why, madam, do you give such words as these
                 To a constable and justice of peace?   735

---

713. *the Rose*] a tavern in Russell Street, Covent Garden, adjoining
Drury Lane Theatre. It is supposedly the scene of the orgy in the third
picture of Hogarth's *Rake's Progress* (1735).

719. *common shores*] that is, open channels full of refuse, one of the horrors
of London life in the eighteenth century.

I fancy you'll better know how to speak
By that time you've been in Bridewell a week,
  Have beaten good hemp, and been
    Whipped at a post;
  I hope you'll repent when some skin   740
    You have lost.
But if this makes you tremble, I'll not be severe,
Come down a good guinea and you shall be clear.

NOVEL.

Oh, Mr. Murdertext, you I am sure are the commander in
this enterprise. If you will prevent the rest of our show, let 745
me beg you will permit the dance.

AIR XXIII, *Charming Betty*

    Gentle preacher,
    Non-con teacher,
  Prithee let us take a dance.
    Leave your canting,   750
    Zealous ranting,
  Come and shake a merry haunch.
    Motions firing,
    Sounds inspiring,
  We are led to softer joys.   755
    Where in trances
    Each soul dances,
  Music then seems only noise.

MURDERTEXT.

Verily I am conquered. Pity prevaileth over severity, and
the flesh hath subdued the spirit. I feel a motion in me, and 760
whether it be of grace or no I am not certain. Pretty maid,
I cannot be deaf any longer to your prayers. I will abide
the performing a dance, and will myself, being thereto
moved by an inward working, accompany you therein,
taking for my partner that reverend gentleman.   765

LUCKLESS.

Then strike up.

---

739. *Whipped at a post*] usual punishment of convicted prostitutes in
Bridewell prison.

Enter Witmore, Mrs. Moneywood, Harriot, *and* Bantomite.

HARRIOT.

　　My dear Harry!

WITMORE.

　　Long live His Majesty of Bantam!

MONEYWOOD.

　　Heaven preserve him!

BANTOMITE.

　　Your gracious father, sir, greets you well.   770

LUCKLESS.

　　What in the devil's name is the meaning of this?

BANTOMITE.

　　I find he is entirely ignorant of his father.

WITMORE.

　　Aye, sir, it is very common in this country for a man not to
　　know his father.

LUCKLESS.

　　What do you mean?   775

BANTOMITE.

　　His features are much altered.

LUCKLESS.

　　Sir, I shall alter your features, if you proceed.

BANTOMITE.

　　Give me leave to explain myself. I was your tutor in your ear-
　　liest years, sent by your father, his present Majesty Francis
　　IV, King of Bantam, to show you the world. We arrived 780
　　at London, when one day among other frolics our ship's crew
　　shooting the bridge, the boat overset, and of all our com-
　　pany I and your royal self were only saved by swimming into

---

　　768. *Long . . . Bantam!*] The conclusion of *The Author's Farce* frequently
received separate mention in bills as "The Triumphs of the King of Bantam." Bantam in Java had long been considered an exotic place of incredible
wealth, and its king had served for the jests of earlier dramatists: in Jonson's
Alchemist Sir Epicure Mammon is promised that he shall be king of Bantam
(II.iii), while in Congreve's *Love for Love* Sir Sampson Legend tells Foresight,
"I have made a cuckold of a King, and the present majesty of *Bantam* is the
issue of these Loins" (II.v). Fielding's purpose, of course, is to make his
denouement as incredible as possible, and a more fantastic series of un-
motivated discoveries which reveal unsuspected relationships in ludicrous
scenes of recognition would be hard to imagine.

Billingsgate. But though I saved my life, I lost for some
time my senses, and you, as I then feared, forever. When I 785
recovered, after a long fruitless search for my royal master,
I set sail for Bantam, but was driven by the winds on far
distant coasts and wandered several years, till at last I
arrived once more at Bantam. Guess how I was received:
the king ordered me to be imprisoned for life. At last some 790
lucky chance brought thither a merchant, who offered this
jewel as a present to the King of Bantam.

LUCKLESS.

Ha! It is the same which was tied upon my arm, which by
good luck I preserved from every other accident till want of
money forced me to pawn it. 795

BANTOMITE.

The merchant, being strictly examined, said he had it of a
pawnbroker, upon which I was immediately dispatched to
England, and the merchant kept close prisoner till my
return, then to be punished with death, or rewarded with
the government of an island. 800

LUCKLESS.

Know then, that at that time when you lost your senses I
also lost mine. I was taken up half dead by a waterman
and conveyed to his wife, who sold oysters, by whose
assistance I recovered. But the waters of the Thames, like
those of Lethe, had caused an entire oblivion of my former 805
fortune. But now it breaks in like light upon me, and I begin
to recollect it all. Is not your name Gonsalvo?

BANTOMITE.

It is.

LUCKLESS.

Oh, my Gonsalvo! ⎫
BANTOMITE. ⎬ *Embrace.*
Oh, my dearest lord! ⎭ 810

791–792. *this jewel*] The best-known recent play in which the solution of
the plot hinged on the identification of a piece of jewelry was probably
Steele's *The Conscious Lovers*, 1722.

807. *Is . . . Gonsalvo?*] Several of Dryden's plays have recognition scenes
rather like this, but the name Gonsalvo suggests that Fielding was thinking
particularly of the concluding scene of *The Rival Ladies* (1664), especially
since he quotes a speech from the same scene in the last note of *The Tragedy
of Tragedies*.

LUCKLESS.

But say by what lucky accident you discovered me.

BANTOMITE.

I did intend to have advertised you in the *Evening Post* with a reward, but being directed by the merchant to the pawn-broker, I was accidentally there inquiring after you when your boy brought your nab. Oh, sad remembrance, that the 815 son of a king should pawn a hat! The woman told me, that was the boy that pawned the jewel, and of him I learned where you lodged.

LUCKLESS.

Prodigious fortune!   *A posthorn without.*

Enter Messenger.

MESSENGER.

An express is arrived from Bantam with the news of His 820 Majesty's death.

BANTOMITE.

Then, sir, you are king. Long live Henry I, King of Bantam!

OMNES.

Long live Henry I, King of Bantam!

LUCKLESS.

Witmore, I now may repay your generosity.

WITMORE.

Fortune has repaid me, I am sure more than she owed, by 825 conferring this blessing on you.

LUCKLESS.

My friend. But here I am indebted to the golden goddess for having given me an opportunity to aggrandize the mistress of my soul and set her on the throne of Bantam. So once more repeat your acclamations, Long live Henry and 830 Harriot, King and Queen of Bantam!

OMNES.

Huzza!

AIR XXIV, *Gently Touch the Warbling Lyre*

HARRIOT.   Let others fondly court a throne,
                  All my joy's in you alone;

---

815. *nab*] "the *Nab* or Trencher Hat, with the Brim flapping over their Eyes . . ." (*Jonathan Wild*, II, chap. 6).

	Let me find a crown in you,	835
	Let me find a scepter too;	
	Equal in the court or grove	
	I am blest, do you but love.	
LUCKLESS.	Were I not with you to live,	
	Bantam would no pleasure give.	840
	Happier in some forest I	
	Could upon that bosom lie.	
	I would guard you from all harms	
	While you slept within my arms.	
HARRIOT.	Would an Alexander rise,	845
	Him I'd view with scornful eyes.	
LUCKLESS.	Would Helen with thy charms compare,	
	Her I'd think not half so fair.	
	Dearest shalt thou ever be.	
HARRIOT.	Thou alone shalt reign in me.	850

CONSTABLE.

I hope your majesty will pardon a poor, ignorant constable. I did not know your worship, I assure you.

LUCKLESS.

Pardon you? Aye more, you shall be chief constable of Bantam. You, Mr. Murdertext, shall be my chaplain; you, sir, my orator; you my poet laureate; you my bookseller; 855 you, Don Tragedio, Sir Farcical, and Signior Opera, shall entertain the city of Bantam with your performances; Mrs. Novel, you shall be a romance writer; and to show my generosity, Marplay and Sparkish shall superintend my theaters. All proper servants for the King of Bantam. 860

MONEYWOOD.

I always thought he had something more than ordinary in him.

LUCKLESS.

This gentlewoman is the Queen's mother.

MONEYWOOD.

For want of a better, gentlemen.

AIR XXV, *Oh Ponder Well*

Alack, how altered is my fate, 865
What changes have I seen.
For I, who lodgings let of late,
Am now again a queen.

PUNCH.

> And I who in this puppet show
> Have played Punchinello   870
> Will now let all the audience know
> I am no common fellow.

If his Majesty of Bantam will give me leave, I can make a discovery which will be to his satisfaction. You have chose for a wife Henrietta, Princess of Old Brentford.   875

OMNES.

How!

PUNCH.

When the King of Old Brentford was expelled by the King of the New, the Queen flew away with her little daughter, then about two years old, and was never heard of since. But I sufficiently recollect the phiz of my mother, and thus 880 I ask her blessing.

MONEYWOOD.

Oh, my son!

HARRIOT.

Oh, my brother!

PUNCH.

Oh, my sister!

MONEYWOOD.

I am sorry, in this pickle, to remember who I am. But, 885 alas, too true is all you've said. Though I have been reduced to let lodgings, I was the Queen of Brentford, and this, though a player, is a king's son.

Enter Joan.

JOAN.

Then I am a king's daughter, for this gentleman is my husband.   890

MONEYWOOD.

My daughter!

HARRIOT, LUCKLESS.

My sister!

---

877. *Old Brentford*] Naturally the two Kings of Brentford in *The Rehearsal* must have had queens, as Durfey implied when he entitled an unacted burlesque *The Two Queens of Brentford* (1721). Only a Queen of Brentford could produce a flesh-and-blood princess and a puppet as offspring.

PUNCH.

My wife!

LUCKLESS.

Strike up, kettledrums and trumpets. Punch, I will restore
you into your kingdom at the expense of my own. I will 895
send an express to Bantam for my army.

PUNCH.

Brother, I thank you. And now, if you please, we will
celebrate these happy discoveries with a dance.   *A dance.*

LUCKLESS.

Taught by my fate, let never bard despair,
Though long he drudge and feed on Grub Street air,   900
Since him, at last, 'tis possible to see
As happy and as great a king as me.

EPILOGUE

1 POET	Mr. Jones
2 POET	Mr. Dove
3 POET	Mr. Marshall
4 POET	Mr. Wells, Jr.
PLAYER	Miss Palms
CAT	Mrs. Martin

Four Poets *sitting at a table.*

1 POET.　Brethren, we are assembled here to write
An epilogue which must be spoke tonight.

2 POET.　Let the first lines be to the pit addressed.

3 POET.　If critics too were mentioned it were best.
With fulsome flattery let them be crammed.　　5
But if they damn the play—

1 POET.　　　　　　　　　　—let them be damned.

2 POET.　Supposing therefore, brother, we should lay
Some very great encomiums on the play?

3 POET.　It cannot be amiss.

1 POET.　　　　　　　　Now mount the boxes,
Abuse the beaus and complement the doxies.　　10

4 POET.　Abuse the beaus! But how?

1 POET.　　　　　　　　　　Oh, never mind. ⎫
In every modern epilogue you'll find　　　　　⎬
Enough which we may borrow of that kind. ⎭

3 POET.　What will the name of imitation soften?

1 POET.　Oh, sir, you cannot say good things too often.　　15
And sure those thoughts which in another shine
Become not duller by becoming mine.

3 POET.　I'm satisfied.

1 POET.　　　　　　The audience is already
Divided into critic, beau, and lady;
Nor box, nor pit, nor gallery can show　　20
One who's not lady, critic, or a beau.

3 POET.　It must be very difficult to please
Fancies so odd, so opposite as these.

1 POET.　The task is not so difficult as put:
There's one thing pleases all.

2 POET.	What is that?
1 POET.	Smut. 25

For as a whore is liked for being tawdry,
So is an epilogue for—

3 POET (*in a passion*).   I order you,
On pain of my departure, not to chatter
One word so very savory of the creature.
For, by my pen, might I Parnassus share,   30
I'd not to gain it all offend the fair.

1 POET.   You are too nice. For say whate'er we can,
Their modesty is safe behind a fan.

4 POET.   Well, let us now begin.

3 POET.   But we omit
An epilogue's chief decoration, wit.   35

1 POET.   It hath been so, but that stale custom's broken;
Though dull to read, 'twill please you when 'tis spoken.

Enter Luckless.

LUCKLESS.   Fie, gentlemen, the audience now hath stayed
This half hour for the epilogue.

ALL POETS.   'Tis not made.

LUCKLESS.   How! Then I value not your aid of that,   40
I'll have the epilogue spoken by a cat.
Puss, puss, puss, puss, puss, puss, puss.

Enter Cat.

1 POET.   I'm in a rage.
When cats come on, poets should leave the stage.
                          Exeunt Poets.

CAT.   Mew, mew.

LUCKLESS.   Poor puss, come hither pretty rogue. ⎫
Who knows but you may come to be in vogue? ⎬   45
Some ladies like a cat, and some a dog. ⎭

Enter a Player.

PLAYER.   Cass, cass, cass, cass! Fie, Mr. Luckless, what
Can you be doing with that filthy cat?   *Exit* Cat.

LUCKLESS.   Oh, curst misfortune! What can I be doing?
This devil's coming in has proved my ruin.   50
She's driven the cat and epilogue away.

−79−

PLAYER.   Sure you are mad and know not what you say.

LUCKLESS. Mad you may call me, madam; but you'll own,
           I hope, I am not madder than the town.

PLAYER.   A cat to speak an epilogue!

LUCKLESS.   Speak! No,   55
           Only to act the epilogue in dumb show.

PLAYER.   Dumb show!

AUTHOR.   Why, pray, is that so strange a comedy?
           And have you not seen Perseus and Andromeda,
           Where you may find strange incidents intended
           And regular intrigues begun and ended,   60
           Though not a word doth from an actor fall? ⎫
           As 'tis polite to speak in murmurs small,   ⎬
           Sure, 'tis politer not to speak at all.   ⎭

PLAYER.   But who is this?

Enter Cat *as a woman.*

AUTHOR.   I know her not.

CAT.   I that
           Am now a woman, lately was a cat.   65
                                        Turns to the audience.
           Gallants, you seem to think this transformation
           As strange as was the rabbit's procreation,
           That 'tis as odd a cat should take the habit
           Of breeding us as we should breed a rabbit.
           I'll warrant eating one of them would be   70
           As easy to a beau as—kissing me.
           I would not for the world that thing should catch us,
           Cries scared Sir Plume. Fore gad, my lord, she'd
                 scratch us.

---

58. *Perseus and Andromeda*] Although there were several pantomimes with
this title, the reference is undoubtedly to the entertainment composed by
Theobald for Rich which first appeared at Lincoln's Inn Fields on Jan 2,
1730; it had great success and was in fact staged on the same night that
The Author's Farce opened at the Haymarket. At one point in this performance Rich appeared in the shape of a dog, and this dog may have
suggested Fielding's cat.

67. *the rabbit's procreation*] In November, 1726, Mary Toft (or Tofts) of
Godalming in Surrey pretended to give birth to a litter of rabbits. The
credulity displayed, even by doctors, made this memorable enough that
today she has a place in the *Dictionary of National Biography*.

Yet let not that deter you from your sport,
You'll find my nails are pared exceeding short. 75
But, ha, what murmurs through the benches roam!
The husbands cry, we've cat enough at home.
This transformation can be strange to no man;
There's a great likeness 'twixt a cat and woman.

Changed by her lover's earnest prayers, we're told, 80
A cat was, to a beauteous maid of old.
Could modern husbands thus the gods prevail on,
Oh gemini! What wife would have no tail on?
Puss would be seen where madam lately sat,
And every Lady Townley be a cat. 85

Say, all of you, whose honeymoon is over,
What would you give such changes to discover,
And waking in the morn, instead of bride,
To find poor pussy purring by your side?
Say, gentle husbands, which of you would curse, 90
And cry, my wife is altered for the worse?

Should to our sex the gods like justice show,
And at our prayers transform our husbands too,
Many a lord who now his fellows scorns
Would then exceed a cat by nothing—but his horns. 95
So plenty then would be those foes to rats,
Henley might prove that all mankind are cats.

FINIS

80–81. *Changed . . . was*] a fable from Aesop to which Fielding also
alludes in *Tom Jones*, XII, chap. 5; Prior had used it in "To my Lord
Buckhurst, Very Young, Playing with a Cat."

Appendix A

The Revision of The Author's Farce

[For the Drury Lane production of 1734 Fielding revised his entire play. Only scenes added or recast are given here.

The scene between Luckless and Harriot was reworded, perhaps to provide a better scene for Mrs. Clive, the new Harriot.]

[I.iii]   Luckless, Harriot.

LUCKLESS.

Dear Harriot!

HARRIOT.

I have waited an opportunity to return to you.

LUCKLESS.

Oh, my dear, I am so sick.

HARRIOT.

What's the matter?

LUCKLESS.

Oh, your mother, your mother!

HARRIOT.

What, has she been scolding ever since?

LUCKLESS.

Worse, worse!

HARRIOT.

Heaven forbid she should threaten to go to law with you.

LUCKLESS.

Oh, worse, worse! She threatens to go to church with me. She has made me a generous offer, that if I will but marry her, she will suffer me to settle all she has upon her.

HARRIOT.

Generous creature! Sure you will not resist the proposal?

LUCKLESS.

Hum! What would you advise me to?

HARRIOT.

>Oh, take her, take her, by all means. You will be the prettiest, finest, loveliest, sweetest couple. Auh! What a delicate dish of matrimony you will make. Her age with your youth, her avarice with your extravagance, and her scolding with your poetry.

LUCKLESS.

>Nay, but I am serious and I desire you would be so. You know my unhappy circumstances and your mother's wealth. It would be at least a prudent match.

HARRIOT.

>Oh, extremely prudent, ha, ha, ha! The world will say, Lard, who could have thought Mr. Luckless had had so much prudence. This one action will overbalance all the follies of your life.

LUCKLESS.

>Faith, I think it will. But, dear Harriot, how can I think of losing you forever? And yet as our affairs stand, I see no possibility of our being happy together. It will be some pleasure too that I may have it in my power to serve you. Believe me, it is with the utmost reluctance I think of parting with you. For if it was in my power to have you—

HARRIOT.

>Oh, I am very much obliged to you. I believe you. Yes, you need not swear; I believe you.

LUCKLESS.

>And can you as easily consult prudence and part with me? For I would not buy my own happiness at the price of yours.

HARRIOT.

>I thank you, sir. Part with you! Intolerable vanity!

LUCKLESS.

>Then I am resolved, and so, my good landlady, have at you!

HARRIOT.

>Stay, sir, let me acquaint you with one thing: you are a villain. And don't think I'm vexed at anything but that I should have been such a fool as ever to have had a good opinion of you.   *Crying.*

LUCKLESS.

>Ha, ha, ha! Caught, by Jupiter! And did my dear Harriot think me in earnest?

HARRIOT.

And was you not in earnest?

LUCKLESS.

What, to part with thee? A pretty woman will be sooner in earnest to part with her beauty, or a great man with his power.

HARRIOT.

I wish I were assured of the sincerity of your love.

[Then follows the Air to the tune of Buttered Pease and the scene concludes much as in the earlier version. The next major change is the insertion of a new scene after the Luckless-Witmore scene to introduce Theophilus Cibber as Marplay, Jr. (Aspects of Fielding's satire on him are discussed in Appendix B.)]

[I.vi]   Luckless, Witmore, Marplay, Jr.

MARPLAY, JR.

Mr. Luckless, I kiss your hands. Sir, I am your most obedient humble servant. You see, Mr. Luckless, what power you have over me. I attend your commands, though several persons of quality have stayed at court for me above this hour.

LUCKLESS.

I am obliged to you. I have a tragedy for your house, Mr. Marplay.

MARPLAY, JR.

Ha! If you will send it to me, I will give you my opinion of it, and if I can make any alterations in it that will be for its advantage, I will do it freely.

WITMORE.

Alterations, sir?

MARPLAY, JR.

Yes, sir, alterations. I will maintain it, let a play be never so good, without alteration it will do nothing.

WITMORE.

Very odd indeed.

MARPLAY, JR.

Did you ever write, sir?

WITMORE.

No, sir, I thank heaven.

MARPLAY, JR.

Oh, your humble servant, your very humble servant, sir. When you write yourself, you will find the necessity of alterations. Why, sir, would you guess that I had altered Shakespeare?

WITMORE.

Yes faith, sir, no one sooner.

MARPLAY, JR.

Alackaday! Was you to see the plays when they are brought to us, a parcel of crude, undigested stuff. We are the persons, sir, who lick them into form, that mould them into shape. The poet make the play, indeed! The color man might be as well said to make the picture, or the weaver the coat. My father and I, sir, are a couple of poetical tailors. When a play is brought us, we consider it as a tailor does his coat, we cut it, sir, we cut it. And let me tell you, we have the exact measure of the town, we know how to fit their taste. The poets, between you and me, are a pack of ignorant—

WITMORE.

Hold, hold, sir. This is not quite so civil to Mr. Luckless. Besides, as I take it, you have done the town the honor of writing yourself.

MARPLAY, JR.

Sir, you are a man of sense and express yourself well. I did, as you say, once make a small sally into Parnassus, took a sort of flying leap over Helicon. But if ever they catch me there again! Sir, the town have a prejudice to my family, for if any play could have made them ashamed to damn it, mine must. It was all over plot. It would have made half a dozen novels. Nor was it crammed with a pack of wit-traps like Congreve and Wycherley, where everyone knows when the joke was coming. I defy the sharpest critic of 'em all to have known when any jokes of mine were coming. The dialogue was plain, easy, and natural, and not one single joke in it from the beginning to the end. Besides, sir, there was one scene of tender, melancholy conversation, enough to have melted a heart of stone; and yet they damned it. And they damned themselves, for they shall have no more of mine.

WITMORE.

Take pity on the town, sir.

MARPLAY, JR.

I! No, sir, no, I'll write no more. No more, unless I am forced to it.

LUCKLESS.

That's no easy thing, Marplay.

MARPLAY, JR.

Yes, sir. Odes, odes, a man may be obliged to write those, you know.

LUCKLESS, WITMORE.

Ha, ha, ha! That's true indeed.

LUCKLESS.

But about my tragedy, Mr. Marplay?

MARPLAY, JR.

I believe my father is at the playhouse. If you please, we will read it now, but I must call on a young lady first. —Hey! Who's there? Is my footman there? Order my chair to the door. —Your servant, gentlemen. —*Caro vien.*

Exit singing.

WITMORE.

This is the most finished gentleman I ever saw, and hath not, I dare swear, his equal.

LUCKLESS.

If he has, here he comes.

[As Marplay, Jr., leaves singing the fashionable aria from Handel's *Porus*, Bookweight enters, and Act I continues as in the earlier version. In the opening scenes of Act II Marplay, Jr., takes the place of Sparkish. Since Wilks had died in 1732, some revision would have been needed in any case.]

[II.i]   *The playhouse.*
            Luckless, Marplay, Sr., Marplay, Jr.

LUCKLESS (*reads*).

Then hence my sorrows, hence my every fear,
No matter where, so we are blessed together.
With thee, the barren rocks, where not one step
Of human race lies printed in the snow,
Look lovely as the smiling infant spring.

MARPLAY, SR.

Augh! Will you please to read that again, sir?

LUCKLESS.

Then hence my sorrow, hence my every fear.

MARPLAY, SR.

Then hence my sorrow . . . Horror is a much better word. And then in the second line, *No matter where, so we are blessed together*; undoubtedly it should be, *No matter where, so somewhere we're together.* Where is the question, somewhere is the answer. Read on, sir.

LUCKLESS.

With thee, etc.

MARPLAY, SR.

No, no, I could alter those lines to a much better idea.
With thee, the barren blocks where not a bit
Of human face is painted on the bark,
Look green as Covent Garden in the spring.

LUCKLESS.

Green as Covent Garden!

MARPLAY, JR.

Yes, yes, Covent Garden Market, where they sell greens.

LUCKLESS.

Monstrous!

MARPLAY, SR.

Pray, sir, read on.

LUCKLESS.

Leandra: *Oh my Harmonio, I could hear thee still;*
The nightingale to thee sings out of tune.
While on thy faithful breast my head reclines
The downy pillow's hard. While from thy lips
I drink delicious draughts of nectar down,
Falernian wines seem bitter to my taste.

MARPLAY, JR.

Here's meat, drink, singing, and lodging, egad.

LUCKLESS.

He answers:

MARPLAY, JR.

But, sir—

LUCKLESS.

Oh let me pull thee, press thee to my heart,
Thou rising spring of everlasting sweets.

Take notice, Fortune, I forgive thee all,
Thou'st made Leandra mine. Thou flood of joy
Mix with my soul, and rush through every vein.

MARPLAY, SR.

Those last two lines again, if you please.

LUCKLESS.

Thou'st made, etc.

MARPLAY, JR.

Thou flood of joy
Mix with my soul, and rush through every vein.

Those are two excellent lines indeed; I never writ better myself. But, sar—

LUCKLESS.

Leandra's mine. Go bid the tongue of fate
Pronounce another word of bliss like that.
Search through the eastern mines and golden shores
Where lavish nature pours forth all her stores;
For to my lot could all her treasures fall,
I would not change Leandra for 'em all.

There ends act the first, and such an act, as I believe, never was on this stage yet.

MARPLAY, JR.

Nor never will, I hope.

MARPLAY, SR.

Pray, sir, let me look at one thing:
Falernian wines seem bitter to my taste.

Pray, sir, what sort of wines may your Falernian be? For I never heard of 'em before; and I am sure, as I keep the best company, if there had been such sorts of wines I should have tasted 'em. Tokay I have drank, and Lacrimae I have drank, but what your Falernian is, the devil take me if I can tell.

MARPLAY, JR.

I fancy, father, these wines grow at the top of Parnassus.

LUCKLESS.

Do they so, Mr. Pert? Why then I fancy you have never tasted them.

MARPLAY, SR.

Suppose you should say, The wines of Cape are bitter to my taste.

LUCKLESS.

Sir, I cannot alter it.

MARPLAY, SR.

Nor we cannot act it. It won't do, sir, and so you need give yourself no farther trouble about it.

LUCKLESS.

What particular fault do you find?

MARPLAY, JR.

Sar, there is nothing that touches me, nothing that is coercive to my passions.

LUCKLESS.

Fare you well, sir. May another play be coercive to your passions. [*Exit.*]

[II.ii]   Marplay, Sr., Marplay, Jr.

MARPLAY, SR.

Ha, ha, ha!

MARPLAY, JR.

What do you think of the play?

MARPLAY, SR.

It may be a very good one for aught I know; but I am resolved, since the town will not receive any of mine, they shall have none from any other. I'll keep them to their old diet.

MARPLAY, JR.

But suppose they won't feed on't?

MARPLAY, SR.

Then it shall be crammed down their throats.

MARPLAY, JR.

I wish, father, you would leave me that art for a legacy, since I am afraid I am like to have no other from you.

MARPLAY, SR.

'Tis buff, child, 'tis buff, true Corinthian brass; and heaven be praised, though I have given thee no gold I have given thee enough of that, which is the better inheritance of the two. Gold thou mighst have spent, but this is a lasting estate that will stick by thee all thy life.

MARPLAY, JR.

What shall be done with that farce which was damned last night?

MARPLAY, SR.

Give it to 'em again tomorrow. I have told some persons of
quality that it is a good thing, and I am resolved not to
be in the wrong. Let us see which will be weary first, the
town of damning or we of being damned.

MARPLAY, JR.

Rat the town, I say.

MARPLAY, SR.

That's a good boy, and so say I. But prithee, what didst
thou do with the comedy which I gave thee t'other day,
that I thought a good one?

MARPLAY, JR.

Did as you ordered me, returned it to the author and told
him it would not do.

MARPLAY, SR.

You did well. If thou writest thyself, and that I know thou
art very well qualified to do, it is thy interest to keep back all
other authors of any merit, and be as forward to advance
those of none.

MARPLAY, JR.

But I am a little afraid of writing; for my writings, you
know, have fared but ill hitherto.

MARPLAY, SR.

That is because thou hast a little mistaken the method of
writing. The art of writing, boy, is the art of stealing old
plays by changing the name of the play, and new ones by
changing the name of the author.

MARPLAY, JR.

If it was not for these cursed hisses and catcalls—

MARPLAY, SR.

Harmless music, child, very harmless music, and what,
when one is but well seasoned to it, has no effect at all.
For my part I have been used to 'em.

MARPLAY, JR.

Aye, and I have been used to 'em too, for that matter.

MARPLAY, SR.

And stood 'em bravely too. Idle young actors are fond of
applause, but take my word for it, a clap is a mighty silly
empty thing and does no more good than a hiss; and
therefore if any man loves hissing, he may have his three
shillings worth at me whenever he pleases.   *Exeunt.*

[The scenes in Bookweight's house received some topical additions, but there are no major changes until the end of the act. Mrs. Clive, the Harriot, was also to play Mrs. Novel in the puppet show. There was necessarily a great deal of doubling of parts between farce and puppet show, and in this case Fielding made it, if only slightly, part of his plot material. This invited further rearrangement and a more gradual introduction of the Bantam theme.]

[II.x]   Luckless, Harriot.

LUCKLESS.

Dear Harriot!

HARRIOT.

I was going to the playhouse to look after you. I am frightened out of my wits. I have left my mother at home with the strangest sort of man who is inquiring after you. He has raised a mob before the door by the oddity of his appearance; his dress is like nothing I ever saw, and he talks of Kings, and Bantam, and the strangest stuff.

LUCKLESS.

What the devil can he be?

HARRIOT.

One of your old acquaintance, I suppose, in disguise; one of His Majesty's officers with his commission in his pocket, I warrant him.

LUCKLESS.

Well, but have you your part perfect?

HARRIOT.

I had, unless this fellow hath frightened it out of my head again. But I am afraid I shall play it wretchedly.

LUCKLESS.

Why so?

HARRIOT.

I shall never have assurance enough to go through with it, especially if they should hiss me.

LUCKLESS.

Oh, your mask will keep you in countenance, and as for hissing, you need not fear it. The audience are generally so favorable to young beginners. But hist, here is your mother and she has seen us. Adieu, my dear, make what haste you can to the playhouse.   *Exit.*

[II.xi]   Harriot, Moneywood.

HARRIOT.

I wish I could avoid her, for I suppose we shall have an alarum.

MONEYWOOD.

So, so, very fine; always together, always caterwauling. How like a hangdog he stole off. And it's well for him he did, for I should have rung such a peal in his ears. There's a friend of his at my house would be very glad of his company, and I wish it was in my power to bring 'em together.

HARRIOT.

You would not surely be so barbarous.

MONEYWOOD.

Barbarous, ugh! You whining, puling fool! Hussy, you have not a drop of my blood in you. What, you are in love, I suppose?

HARRIOT.

If I was, madam, it would be no crime.

MONEYWOOD.

Yes, madam, but it would, and a folly too. No woman of sense was ever in love with anything but a man's pocket. What, I suppose he has filled your head with a pack of romantic stuff of streams and dreams and charms and arms. I know this is the stuff they all run on with, and so run into our debts and run away with our daughters. Come, confess, are not you two to live in a wilderness together on love? Ah, thou fool, thou wilt find he will pay thee in love just as he has paid me in money. If thou wert resolved to go a-begging, why did you not follow the camp? There indeed you might have carried a knapsack, but here you will have no knapsack to carry. There indeed you might have had the chance of burying half a score husbands in a campaign, whereas a poet is a long-lived animal; you have but one chance of burying him, and that is starving him.

HARRIOT.

Well, madam, and I would sooner starve with the man I love than ride in a coach and six with him I hate. And as for his passion, you will not make me suspect that, for he hath given me such proofs on't.

MONEYWOOD.

Proofs! I shall die. Has he given you proofs of love?

HARRIOT.

All that any modest woman can require.

MONEYWOOD.

If he has given you all a modest woman can require, I am afraid he has given you more than a modest woman should take. Because he has been so good a lodger, I suppose I shall have some more of the family to keep. It is probable I shall live to see half a dozen grandsons of mine in Grub Street.

[II.xii]   Moneywood, Harriot, Jack.

JACK.

Oh, madam, the man whom you took for a bailiff is certainly some great man. He has a vast many jewels and other fine things about him. He offered me twenty guineas to show him my master, and has given away so much money among the chairmen that some folks believe he intends to stand member of parliament for Westminster.

MONEYWOOD.

Nay, then I am sure he is worth inquiring into. So, d'ye hear, sirrah, make as much haste as you can before me, and desire him to part with no more money till I come.

[*Exeunt* Moneywood, Jack.]

HARRIOT.

So, now my mother is in pursuit of money, I may securely go in pursuit of my lover, and I am mistaken, good mamma, if e'en you would not think that the better pursuit of the two.

In generous love transporting raptures lie,
Which age, with all its treasures, cannot buy.

[Cibber's appointment to the laureateship in 1730 suggested a change in the main plot of the puppet show; the love of Nonsense for Signior Opera becomes subordinate to the new theme, the election of an archpoet. This necessitates a new beginning for Act III; Fielding substitutes the Manager for the Player and introduces an actual person, Mr. Seedo, musical director on the Drury Lane staff.]

[III]   *The Playhouse.*
Enter Luckless *as master of the show, and* Manager.

LUCKLESS.

It's very surprising that after I have been at all this expense and trouble in setting my things up in your house you should desire me to recant; and now too, when the spectators are all assembled and will either have the show or their money.

MANAGER.

Nay, sir, I am very ready to perform my covenant with you, but I am told that some of the players do not like their parts and threaten to leave the house, some to the Haymarket, some to Goodman's Fields, and others to set up two or three more new playhouses in several parts of the town.

LUCKLESS.

I have quieted all that, and believe there is not one engaged in the performance but who is now very well satisfied.

MANAGER.

Well, sir, then so am I. But pray what is the design or plot? For I could make neither head nor tail on't.

LUCKLESS.

Why, sir, the chief business is the election of an archpoet, or as others call him a poet laureate, to the Goddess of Nonsense. I have introduced indeed several other characters not entirely necessary to the main design, for I was assured by a very eminent critic that in the way of writing great latitude might be allowed, and that a writer of puppet shows might take as much more liberty than a writer of operas, as an opera writer might be allowed beyond a writer of plays. As for the scene, it lies on the other side of the River Styx, and all the people in my play are dead.

MANAGER.

I wish they may not be damned too, with all my heart.

LUCKLESS.

Sir, I depend much on the good nature of the audience, but they are impatient; I hear them knock with their canes. Let us begin immediately. I think we will have an overture played on this occasion. Mr. Seedo, have you not provided a new overture on this occasion?

SEEDO.

I have composed one.

LUCKLESS.

Then pray let us have it. Come, sir, be pleased to sit down by me.

[The puppet show, with its lack of logical sequence, invited the introduction of new scenes as well as the deletion of scenes that either had succeeded indifferently or had lost their topicality. Despite Luckless's earlier statement that the scene "lies on the other side of the River Styx," it seems that in the revision the characters in the first interlude have not yet crossed the river—one example of the inconsistency introduced in the new version. The first newcomer to the shades is a Director, who enters at line 137, immediately after the scene with the Sexton, his inclusion prompted by the discovery in 1731–1732 of the misconduct of officials of the Charitable Corporation.]

Enter Director.

DIRECTOR.

Mr. Charon, I want a boat to cross the river.

CHARON.

You shall have a place, sir; I believe I have just room for you unless you are a lawyer, and I have strict orders to carry no more over yet: hell is too full of them already.

DIRECTOR.

Sir, I am a director.

CHARON.

A director, what's that?

DIRECTOR.

A director of a company, sir. I am surprised you should not know what that is; I thought our names had been famous enough on this road.

CHARON.

Oh sir, I ask your honor's pardon. Will you be pleased to go aboard?

DIRECTOR.

I must have a whole boat by myself, for I have two wagon loads of treasure that will be here immediately.

CHARON.

It is as much as my place is worth to take anything of that nature aboard.

DIRECTOR.

Pshaw, pshaw, you shall go snacks with me and I warrant we cheat the devil. I have been already too hard for him in the other world. Do you understand what security on bottomry is? I'll make your fortune.

CHARON.

Here, take the gentleman, let him be well fettered and carried aboard. Away with him!

SAILOR.

Sir, here are a wagonload of ghosts arrived from England that were knocked on the head at a late election.

CHARON.

Fit out another boat immediately. But be sure to search their pockets, that they carry nothing over with them. I found a bank bill of fifty pound t'other day in the pocket of a cobbler's ghost who came hither on the same account.

[Here a Second Sailor announces the arrival of Don Tragedio and his group, but not as in the earlier version referring to them as authors. The group has been increased by one, Mynheer Van Treble; though he is once addressed his answer is missing—obviously an oversight in the text. In all probability that character made some reference to the two opera companies that were competing at the King's Theatre and Lincoln's Inn Fields. Dr. Orator is allowed to state the cause of his death, "A Muggletonian dog stabbed me." The next major change is the replacement of the quadrille game by Punch's account of it, ending with the stale "great man" joke—an early indication of Fielding's drift toward the opposition to Walpole.]

Enter Punch.

PUNCH.

You, fiddler.

LUCKLESS.

Well, Punch, what's the matter now?

PUNCH.

What do you think my wife Joan is about?

LUCKLESS.

Faith, I can't tell.

PUNCH.

Odsbobs, she is got with three women of quality at quadrille.

LUCKLESS.

Quadrille, ha, ha!

PUNCH.

I have taken a resolution to run away from her and set up a trade.

LUCKLESS.

A trade? Why, you have no stock.

PUNCH.

Oh, but I intend to break, cheat my creditors, and so get one.

LUCKLESS.

That bite is too stale, Master Punch.

PUNCH.

Is it? Then I'll e'en turn lawyer. There is no stock required there but a stock of impudence.

LUCKLESS.

Yes, there is a stock of law, without which you will starve at the bar.

PUNCH.

Aye, but I'll get upon the bench; then I shall soon have law enough, for then I can make anything I say to be law.

LUCKLESS.

Hush, you scurrilous rascal.

PUNCH.

Odsbobs, I have hit it now.

LUCKLESS.

What now?

PUNCH.

I have it at last, the rarest trade. Punch, thou art made forever.

LUCKLESS.

What conceit has the fool got in his head now?

PUNCH.

I'll e'en turn parliament man.

LUCKLESS.

Ha, ha, ha! Why, sirrah, thou hast neither interest nor qualification.

PUNCH.

How, not interest? Yes, sir, Punch is very well known to have a very considerable interest in all the corporations in England; and for qualification, if I have no estate of my own, I can borrow one.

LUCKLESS.

This will never do, Master Punch. You must think of something you have a better qualification for.

PUNCH.

Aye, why then I'll turn great man; that requires no qualification whatsoever.

LUCKLESS.

Get you gone, you impudent rogue.

[The puppet show continues with only minor changes until near its end. Sir Farcical's bone and his "paraphonalia" are cut, and so Air XX is dropped. Air XIV has another stanza inserted, continuing the satire on directors, joining with them supercargoes like those of the East India Company who in 1731 were exposed for charging on their invoices considerably more than the true cost of the goods they were escorting from abroad:

> That some directors cheats were,
>> Some have made bold to doubt,
> Did not the supercargo's care
>> Prevent their finding out.
>>> For a cheating, etc.

One added line by Luckless, at the moment when Nonsense gives the chaplet to Signior Opera, converts old material to the new theme: "Gentlemen, observe how Signior Opera is created Archpoet to the Goddess of Nonsense." It is a bit awkward that Signior Opera, who is not a poet at all, is named Archpoet, and Fielding felt that an explanation was needed for not awarding the position to the living Laureate; hence (despite the presence of Sir Farcical) a changed conclusion to the puppet show, immediately following Air XIX, gives a weak excuse for the Laureate's absence. The scene continues by bringing in the opera manager, Heidegger, and further pads Mrs. Clive's part with a new song for Mrs. Novel.]

NONSENSE.

Alas, what mighty noise?

LUCKLESS.

Gentlemen, the next is a messenger.

Enter Messenger.

MESSENGER.

Stay, Goddess, nor with haste the prize bequeath,
A mighty sprite now hastens here beneath;
Long in the world your noble cause he fought;
Your laureate there, your precepts still he taught.
To his great son he leaves that laurel now,
And hastens to receive one here below.

NONSENSE.

I can't revoke my grant, but he
Shall manager of our players be.

LUCKLESS.

The next is Count Ugly from the Opera House in the
Haymarket.

Enter Count Ugly.

NONSENSE.

Too late, O mighty Count, you came.

COUNT.

I ask not for myself, for I disdain
O'er the poor ragged tribe of bards to reign.
Me did my stars to happier fates prefer,
Surintendant des plaisirs d'Angleterre.
If masquerades you have, let those be mine,
But on the Signior let the laurel shine.

TRAGEDIO.

What is thy plea? Hast written?

COUNT.   No, nor read.

But if from dullness any may succeed,
To that and nonsense I good title plead,
Naught else was ever in my masquerade.

NONSENSE.

No more. By Styx I swear
That Opera the crown shall wear.

AIR

NOVEL.   Away each meek pretender flies;
                Opera, thou hast gained the prize.
                Nonsense grateful still must own,
                Thou best supportst her throne.

For her subscriptions thou didst gain
By thy soft alluring strain,
When Shakespeare's thought
And Congreve's brought
Their aids to sense in vain.

Beauties who subdue mankind,
Thy soft chains alone can bind.
See within their lovely eyes
The melting wish arise.
While thy sounds enchant the ear,
Lovers think the nymph sincere,
    And projectors
    And directors
Lose a while their fear.

[Here Charon enters to announce the Constable, who enters accompanied by Sir John Bindover, the latter replacing Murdertext of the earlier version. This change, obviously prompted by Fielding's desire to soften the religious satire, shortens the scene; Sir John gets no new lines but keeps those assigned to Murdertext that remain remotely appropriate to a layman. The audience may have identified Sir John with Sir John Gonson, the harlot-hunting Justice of the Peace. Otherwise the conclusion is unchanged save for one technical detail: Harriot is on stage as Mrs. Novel, but one line by Luckless, "Come, madam, now you may lay aside your mask," restores her to her former character.]

Appendix B

The Individuals Represented

COLLEY CIBBER (1671–1757) receives more detailed attention than anyone else represented in *The Author's Farce*. He gets passing mention in I.iv with his name distorted to the German Keyber, as theatrical manager he is Marplay in the opering scenes of Act II, and as comic actor and playwright he is Sir Farcical Comic in Act III. The Marplay scenes concentrate on his arrogance as corrector of plays and on the recent hissing of his pastoral entertainment, *Love in a Riddle*. The same hisses were the cause of Sir Farcical's death, but the satire in the third act centers on Cibber's last major comedy, his revision of Vanbrugh's unfinished *A Journey to London* as *The Provoked Husband*. The incredible English of its preface would have invited satire in any case, but the peculiar gushing praise of the Drury Lane Actors (Mrs. Oldfield "Here *Out-did* her usual *Out-doing*. . . . Perhaps my saying a little more of so memorable an Actress, may give this Play a chance to be read, when the People of this Age shall be Ancestors") gave added motive to the attack.

When *The Author's Farce* was first written Cibber had long been leader of the triumvirate controlling Drury Lane. But Wilks died in 1732 and Booth in 1733, and Cibber sold his share in the patent in the same year. Since Fielding's revised version was written for, not against, Drury Lane and in a totally different climate of theatrical politics, the role of Marplay had to be modified. At the same time, perhaps because the specific jokes based on *The Provoked Husband* were wearing thin, the role of Sir Farcical was shortened. However, Cibber's appointment as Laureate in 1730 offered another opportunity; though he does not reach the stage in this new role, his imminent arrival as one who had long fought in the cause of Nonsense is announced by a messenger.

See R. H. Barker, *Mr. Cibber of Drury Lane* (New York, 1939); Charles B. Woods, "Cibber in Fielding's *Author's Farce:* Three Notes," *Philological Quarterly*, XLIV (1965), 145–151.

THEOPHILUS CIBBER (1703–1758) is absent from the original version of *The Author's Farce*, but changes in theatrical affairs gave him, as Marplay, Jr., the part corresponding to that of Sparkish in Act II and also a completely new scene (I.vi). The younger Cibber had been his father's deputy in the Drury Lane management and presumably expected to succeed him. But with the deaths of Wilks and Booth, Colley Cibber sold his share of the patent to the speculator Highmore. Theophilus withdrew to the Haymarket, taking many of the Drury Lane actors with him. In his revised play Fielding defended the new patentees by attacking Theophilus Cibber, but despite his contribution to their cause, the new patentees were badly beaten and the revolting actors returned to Drury Lane in March, 1734. The portraits of the Marplays in the revised play mark the permanent end of the truce, which had lasted almost two years, between Fielding and the male Cibbers. For these scenes Fielding remembers Theophilus's alteration of Shakespeare (combining II and III *Henry VI*) which achieved only one performance (D.L., July 5, 1723), and his only original full-length play ("A small sally into Parnassus"), the extremely sentimental *The Lover* (D.L., Jan. 20, 1731), which barely escaped damnation. The final reversal belongs to the year 1748, when Theophilus staged the last London performance of *The Author's Farce* in Fielding's lifetime, as a move against Fielding himself (see Introduction, p. xviii).

EDMUND CURLL (1675–1747) was the most notorious publisher of the period; any bookseller introduced into the play could easily suggest him. We have two, Bookweight in the first two acts and Curry, the Bookseller, in the third; the latter's name suggests Curll, and Curry's boast that he has faithfully served the Goddess of Nonsense in this world for thirty years does nothing to deny the identification. The Bookweight of the earlier acts, who keeps a stable of hacks, is presented in more detail; the details fit Curll, but much of this satire is applicable to more than one publisher. Bookweight's forged title pages, his translations from nonexistent foreign originals, and his hiding behind pamphlet publishers like Moore and Smith all suggest Curll; there are references to the pillory and to the Crown Office, with both of which Curll was acquainted. But it is noteworthy that not one word is said of the sensational handling of sexual topics with which Curll's name was often associated, nor of his eagerness to publish biographies, wills, and private papers. In this last respect

Curll's activity increased markedly between 1730 and 1733—"one of the new terrors of death," in Arbuthnot's phrase—and some of Bookweight's lines in the revised version point to this, thereby strengthening the likeness to Curll.

See Ralph Straus, *The Unspeakable Curll* (London, 1927).

SIR JOHN GONSON (*d.* 1765), Justice of the Peace and Chairman of the Westminster Quarter Sessions, was becoming an object of satire. He is twice mentioned (ll. 53, 256) in Pope's "The Fourth Satire of Dr. John Donne" (published anonymously in 1733), and his zeal in hunting harlots gave him place in plate III of Hogarth's *The Harlot's Progress* (1732). A strong enemy of Popery, blasphemy, and profanity, and a member of the Society for the Promotion of Christian Knowledge, he could easily be identified by an audience of 1734 with Sir John Bindover, who takes the place of Murdertext in the original version. Since Fielding wrote no new lines for this role, the identification must rest in part on Sir John's given name and title, and in part on the appropriateness of the lines, once written for a parson, to the zealot magistrate Sir John seems to have been. Since it was thought that Gonson's charges to the jury were written for him by Henley, Sir John Bindover made an admirable dancing partner for Dr. Orator.

ELIZA HAYWOOD (*c.* 1693–1756), who had been pictured in the *Dunciad* (A II, 150) with two babes of love clinging to her waist, seems the obvious person with whom to identify Mrs. Novel. Mrs. Novel is less identified with her art than the others in her group, though what we learn of her life suggests the scandal and sentimentality of fiction. Although she pretends to be a virgin in her first song, she later confesses that she died bearing an illegitimate child. Known principally at this time as a writer of amorous and scandalous prose fiction, Mrs. Haywood was also a dramatist and an actress. It is a curious fact that she performed on the Haymarket stage in a play that caused a brief interruption in the first run of *The Author's Farce*, William Hatchett's *The Rival Father* on April 8 and 9, 1730.

See G. F. Whicher, *The Life and Romances of Mrs. Eliza Haywood* (New York, 1915).

JOHN JAMES HEIDEGGER (*c.* 1659–1749), manager of the Opera in the King's Theatre in the Haymarket, was so notoriously ill-favored that he is instantly recognizable as Count Ugly in the revised version of *The Author's Farce*. Fielding had in 1728 dedicated *The Masquerade* to C–t H–D–R, congratulating him "on that Gift of Nature, by which you seem so adapted to the Post you enjoy. I mean that natural Masque, which is too visible a Perfection to be here insisted on—and, I am sure, never fails of making an impression." Since in the poem itself Heidegger was "toss'd out of Hell" for his ugliness, it is noteworthy that he should in the play be permitted to return there as a supporter of Signior Opera. But the establishment of an opera company in Lincoln's Inn Fields to rival his made opera doubly prominent in the 1733–1734 season and accounts for his appearance near the end of Fielding's revised play. Count Ugly's French title is explained by a footnote in James Bramston's *Art of Politicks* (1731), p. 5: "*All* Mr. Heydegger's *Letters come directed to him from abroad, A* Monsieur, Monsieur Heydegger, Surintendant des Plaisirs d'Angleterre."

JOHN HENLEY (1692–1756) as Dr. Orator receives—at least as far as space goes—more attention than anyone else in the last act of *The Author's Farce*. As the supreme self-advertiser of his time he received constant attention from satirists and is featured in Book II of the *Dunciad*. After resigning his preferment in the Church of England and after (according to the *London Journal*, April 23, 1726) taking "the Oaths required by law to qualify himself as a Baptist Preacher," he established his Oratory in Newport Market, moving in 1729 to Lincoln's Inn Fields near Clare Market. His early projects included ambitious schemes of religious and educational reform, some of which were far from foolish, but he gradually descended to exhibitions of ludicrous "oratory" for which he charged admission. He was early associated secretly with Curll in offers to Robert Walpole, and intermittently from 1730 to 1739 wrote for the *Hyp-Doctor*, a government paper dedicated to ridicule of the opposition. Though several times taken into custody for reckless attacks against church and state he was never brought to trial.

His advertisements best describe him, and hundreds of them appeared in the newspapers over a thirty-year period. One, from the *Daily Post*, for a lecture of October 30, 1728, will suffice here. It will certainly explain Luckless's complaint about the unintelligibility of his advertisements, it reflects on several of Dr. Orator's lines, and it may have inspired the last line of the epilogue: "Henley might prove that all mankind are cats."

At the Desire of some Friends of his Excellency COSSAM COJAH, *Embassador from* Tripoli, *just before they figure all away for the Birth Night.*

At the ORATORY

IN Newport-market, this Evening will be held forth ÆSOP AT MY LORD MAYOR'S SHEW, in a MYSTICO-PIMLICO-FABULISTICO-TRUNDLE-TAIL'D Oration on WHITTINGTON AND HIS CAT— Being a compleat System of Hystory and Observation on Rats and Mice, the singular Invention and Use of Mouse-traps and Baits, the importance and Dignity of a Rat-catcher, and all that Philosophy, and Learning suggest on this sublime and uncommon Topick.

Then Peal XIII of the CHIMES OF THE TIMES, to the Tune of AN OLD COURTIER OF THE KING'S, or ABOUT AND ABOUT, The Game of the World: Wit stirring since last Saturday: On the Ladies powdering before and not behind: The two Muleys: Spaniards very deliberate in Politicks; the Way to hasten them, but whisper that—, and so on to the End of the Chapter.

SAMUEL JOHNSON of Cheshire (1691–1773), dancing master and dramatist, enjoyed spectacular success with his first stage piece, *Hurlothrumbo*, a heroic extravaganza which had a run of thirty-two performances in 1729. Johnson played the part of Lord Flame, sometimes dancing, sometimes walking on stilts, sometimes fiddling, and speaking sometimes in one key, sometimes in another. Though critics called the play a great heap of nonsense and absurdities, it was so popular that Hurlothrumbo societies were formed, and West-minster scholars composed verses in "Hurlothrumbo." The play is referred to in I.v, and near the end of Act III Hurlothrumbo himself is announced by Charon—who cannot quite pronounce his name— but never appears. None of Johnson's other plays had even a normal measure of success, and he stopped writing for the stage in 1741.

JOHN RICH (*c.* 1682–1761), manager of Lincoln's Inn Fields and subsequently of Covent Garden, is now best remembered as producer of *The Beggar's Opera*. Under the stage name of Lun he was the

Harlequin of his age, so that Fielding's Monsieur Pantomime—even though he speaks not a word—would be identified with him. Puns on his name were inevitable; there may be one at the end of Air VIII.

SEEDO [or Sidow or Sydow] (died *c.* 1754) was a German musician resident in England from the 1720's to 1736, affiliated at different times with the Little Theatre in the Haymarket, Drury Lane, and Goodman's Fields. Clearly he was at Drury Lane for the revised version of *The Author's Farce* in 1734, since at the beginning of Act III he speaks *in propria persona*; for this production he certainly contributed the overture and probably the melody for Mrs. Novel's added song, "Away each meek pretender flies." It is quite possible that Seedo was at the Haymarket at the time of the first production, in which case he is to be credited with the entire musical arrangement of *The Author's Farce*. Almost certainly he was associated with Fielding in other ballad operas.

See Walter H. Rubsamen, "Mr. Seedo, Ballad Opera, and the Singspiel," *Miscelánea en homenaje a Monseñor Higinio Anglés* (Barcelona, 1958–1961), II, 775–809; Edgar V. Roberts, "Mr. Seedo's London Career and His Work with Henry Fielding," *Philological Quarterly*, XLV (Jan., 1966).

FRANCESCO BERNARDI SENESINO (*c.* 1680–*c.* 1750), the most famous castrato singer in England from 1720 to 1735, adored by ladies and inevitably the object of satire, is the person an audience of 1730 would be most likely to identify with Signior Opera in Act III. Although the Sailor had identified all in his group as "authors" (a term dropped in the revision), obviously not all were, and nothing suggests that Opera was more than a singer; this would rule out composers like Handel or Bononcini. There are almost no individualizing touches, though his greed may be glanced at in Air VIII. That a castrato should be the father of Mrs. Novel's child need trouble no one in a play in which one ghost almost kills another and in which the heroine turns out to be brother to a puppet.

LEWIS THEOBALD (1688–1744) is honored as a Shakespearean scholar, though the same ability brought him another kind of fame as first hero of Pope's *Dunciad*. But he had also been for many years a Grub Street hack. Among his works were two tragedies, *The Persian*

Princess (D.L., May 31, 1708), and *The Perfidious Brother* (L.I.F., Feb. 21, 1715), both failures, and the prefaces revealed that the failures rankled. Except for dubious Shakespearean adaptations, he thereafter turned to pantomime and opera; of these, *Perseus and Andromeda* (L.I.F., Feb. 1, 1730) is referred to in the epilogue to *The Author's Farce* and at least two others, *The Rape of Proserpine* and *Harlequin a Sorcerer*, are probably glanced at (III, 202, 210). The hero of the *Dunciad* might be expected to appear more prominently, and, even though the identification is hardly obvious to modern readers, Lewis Theobald was probably Fielding's Don Tragedio. The Don, who has long been known at the patent houses (this detail at once eliminates new dramatists like Thomson), once wrote two tragedies especially notable for their nonsense; had they not been hissed he would have written forty by this time. One infers that he is a prolific writer whose memory of early failures has deterred him from producing tragedy in recent years. Other hints are his fondness for thunder and lightning, and for certain peculiarities of style and diction, particularly the inane repetition of words. This last was not so much a characteristic of Theobald's own plays as of his Shakespearean work, where in *Shakespeare Restor'd* he offered to "bring a great number of examples" of this figure—a statement quickly parodied in both text and notes of the *Dunciad*. Parody of tragedy is almost necessarily generic; the identification of Don Tragedio with Theobald is not as precise or necessary to our enjoyment of Fielding as the identification of Dr. Orator or Sir Farcical. Still, Theobald deserves a place at the Court of Nonsense, particularly since his greatest work so far, *Shakespeare Restor'd* (1726), was dedicated to John Rich, also in attendance as Monsieur Pantomime.

See Richard Foster Jones, *Lewis Theobald* (New York, 1919); Charles B. Woods, "Theobald as Fielding's Don Tragedio," *English Language Notes*, II (June, 1965), 266–271.

ROBERT WILKS (1665–1732), the actor who from 1711 until his death was associated with Cibber and Booth in the management of Drury Lane, appears as Sparkish in the first two scenes of the second act. The name is suggested by Wilks' success in dashing comedy roles like Farquhar's Sir Harry Wildair. During the reading of Luckless's play he merely parrots Marplay's comments, just as Wilks was said never to interfere with Cibber's corrections during readings. Fielding admitted that after his return from Leyden "a slight picque" developed between him and Wilks (Preface to *Miscellanies*), and he was sufficiently irritated to change his mind about offering a play—probably *The Temple Beau*—to Drury Lane in which he had hoped to present Wilks in a principal role.

Appendix C

The Tunes

No music was published with the editions of *The Author's Farce*, but all tunes are identified except the specially composed Air XVIII and apart from this one all except Air XVI have been recovered. The versions given here are those published as near to the time of Fielding's play as possible, and minimal adjustments have been made to fit them to Fielding's words.

[I.iii]   Buttered Pease   *anon.*

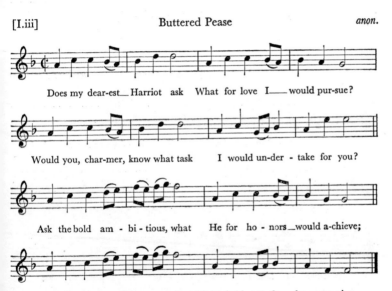

Does my dear-est Harriot ask   What for love I would pur-sue?

Would you, char-mer, know what task   I would un-der - take for you?

Ask the bold am - bi - tious, what   He for ho - nors would a-chieve;

Or the gay   vo - lup - tuous, that Which he'd not for plea-sures give.

[I.iii] Would You the Charming Queen of Love Invite *John Eccles* (?)

Would you the char-ming Queen of__Love In-vite, in-vite with you to dwell, No want your po - ver - ty should prove, No state, no state your ri - ches tell. No want your po - ver-ty should prove, No state, no state__ your ri - ches tell.

[II.iii] **Ye Commons and Peers** *Richard Leveridge*

How un - hap-py's the fate To live by one's pate And be forced to write hack-ney for bread!__ An au-thor's a joke To all man-ner of folk Where - e - ver he pops up his head, his head, Where - e - ver he pops up his head.

ACT III

AIR I   Whilst the Town's Brimful of Folly   *George Monro*

Whilst__the town's brim - ful__ of far - ces, Flock - ing whilst we

see__ her as - ses Thick__as grapes__up - on a bunch, Crit - ics,

whilst__ you smile on mad - ness, And more stu - pid sol - em sad-ness,

Sure__you will__ not frown on Punch. Crit - ics whilst you

smile__on mad - ness, And more stu - pid sol - em sad - ness, Sure you

will__ not frown on Pu————————————————————

---nch. Sure__ you__ will__ not frown__ on Punch.

AIR II   The First of August   *anon.*

Joan, Joan, Joan, has a thun-der-ing tongue, And Joan, Joan,

Joan, is a bold___ one. How hap-py is he Who from wed-lock is

free, For who'd have a wife to___ scold___ one? Joan, Joan,

Joan, has a thun-der-ing tongue, And Joan, Joan, Joan is a bold one.

AIR III   Bobbing Joan   *anon.*

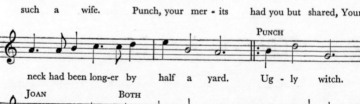

PUNCH

Joan, you are the plague of my life.___ A rope would be welcomer than

JOAN

such a wife. Punch, your mer - its had you but shared, Your

PUNCH

neck had been long-er by half a yard. Ug - ly witch.

JOAN   BOTH

Son of a bitch. Would you were hanged or drowned in a ditch.

AIR IV Silvia, My Dearest *G. F. Handel*

Claps un - i - ver - sal, Ap - plau-ses re - soun - ding, His - ses con -

found-ing At - tend-ing my song.___ My sen-ses drowned___ And I fell

down dead, Whilst I was sing - ing,___ ding, dang, dong. Claps un-i-

ver - sal, Ap - plau-ses re - sound-ing, His - ses con - found-ing At-

tend-ing___my___ song. My sen - ses drowned And I fell down dead,

Whilst I___ was___ sing - ing,___ ding,___ dang, dong.

AIR V   'Twas When the Seas Were Roaring   *G. F. Handel*

Oh! Pit - y all_ a maid - en Con-demned hard fates to prove; I ra - ther would_ have laid_ in Than thus_ have died for love. 'Twas hard___ t'en - count - er death-a Be - fore_the brid - al bed. Ah! Would I had kept__my breath-a And lost___ my maid - en - head.

AIR VI To You Fair Ladies *anon.*

To all you hus - bands and you wives This Punch- i-nel - lo

sings, For re-form - a - tion of your lives This good ad -

vice— he brings: That if you would a - void all ill, You

should leave off— the dear quad - rille. With a fa, la, la,— la

la. That if you would a - void all ill, You should leave—

off— the dear Quad-rille. With a fa, la, la,— la la.

AIR VII   Black Joke   *anon.*

AIR VIII   Lillibolera   *Henry Purcell* (*?*)

Let the fool - ish phil - o - soph - er strive in his cell, By

wis - dom or vir - tue to mer - it true praise, The

sol - dier in hard - ship and dang - er still dwell That

glo - ry and hon - or may crown his last days, The

pa - triot sweat To be thought great, Or

beau - ty all day at the look - ing glass toil, That

pop - u - lar voic - es May ring their ap - plaus - es, While a

breath is the on - ly re - ward of their coil.

AIR IX

Whilst I Gaze on Cloe Trembling *Lewis Ramonden*

May— all— maids— from— me— take— warn - ing

How a lov - er's arms they— fly; Lest— the— first kind—

of - fer— scorn - ing, They, with-out— a sec - ond,— die.

How un-hap - py is my pas-sion! How— tor - ment - ing

is my pain! If you— thwart my in - clin - a - tion,

Let— me die— for love— a - gain.

AIR X   Highland Laddy   *anon.*

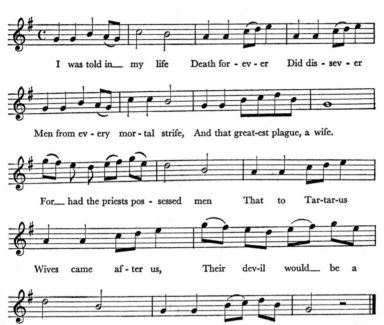

I was told in— my life   Death for - ev - er   Did dis - sev - er

Men from ev - ery mor - tal strife,   And that great-est plague, a wife.

For— had the priests pos - sessed   men   That   to   Tar-tar-us

Wives   came   af - ter us,   Their   dev-il   would— be   a

jest   then,   And   our   dev - il a   wife.

AIR XI

Dusty Miller

anon.

AIR XII — Over the Hills and Far Away — *anon.*

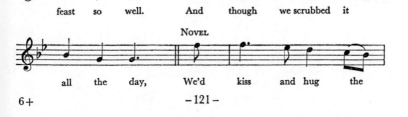

OPERA

Were— I— laid— on— Scot - land's coast, And in— my— arms— em - braced my dear,

Let scrub - a - do do its most, I would know no

NOVEL

grief or fear. Were— we— cast— on Ire - land's soil,

there— con - fined— in bogs to dwell, For

thee po - ta - toes I would boil, No I - rish spouse should

OPERA

feast so well. And though we scrubbed it

NOVEL

all the day, We'd kiss and hug the

6+

night a - way. Scotch and I - rish both should say,

Oh, how__ blest, how blest are they!

AIR XIII   Moll Pately   *anon.*

All   men   are birds   by   na -   ture,

sir, Though they have not wings— to fly; On   earth   a   sol - dier's a

crea   -   ture,   sir,   Much re - sem - bling   a

kite   in   the   sky;   The phy - si - cian is—   a

fowl,   sir,   Whom most— men call— an   owl,   sir,   Who—

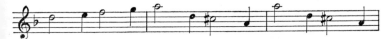

by   his   hoot - ing,   Hoot - ing, hoot - ing,   Hoot - ing, hoot - ing,

Hoot - ing, hoot - ing, Tells us   that death— is   nigh.

AIR XIV   There Was a Jovial Beggar   *anon.*

The stone that all things turns at will to gold, the chem-ist

craves; But gold, with-out the chem - ist's skill, Turns

all men in - to knaves. For a - cheat - ing they will—

go, will go, will go, For a - cheat - ing they will go.

AIR XV   When I Was a Dame of Honor   *Thomas Durfey*

Come all who've heard my cush - ion beat, Con -

fess me as__ full of dull - ness As an - y egg is

full__ of meat Or full moon is of full - ness.

Let the jus - tice and his clerk both own, Than

theirs my dull - ness great - er, And tell__ how I've ha-

rangued the town When I was a bold or - a - tor.

AIR XVII

Be Kind and Love

anon.

[Introduction]

NOVEL

Oh, spare___ to___ take___ his pre - cious life a - way; his pre - cious life a-

way; So sweet___ a___ voice___ mus't sure your___ pas - sion___

[interlude]

lay. Oh, spare___ to

take___ his pre - cious life a - way; So sweet a

voice___ so sweet___ a voice___ so sweet___ a

voice__ must__ sure your pas - sion lay.   Oh, spa---------------------

--re   to   take__ ___

_____   his pre - cious life a - way;   So sweet__   a

voice__   so sweet__   a   voice__   so sweet__   a

voice__ must__ sure your pas-sion lay: must   sure your__ pas - sion

lay:

AIR XIX   Under the Greenwood Tree   *anon.*

In vain a thou - sand her - oes and kings__ Should

court me to their arms, In vain should give me a

thou - sand fine things,__ For thee I'd re - serve my charms.

On that dear breast, en - tranced__ in joys, Oh,

let me ev - er be. Oh, how I will kiss thee,

How I'll em - bliss thee, When thou art a - bed with me__.

6*

AIR XX

Hunt the Squirrel

anon.

Can my God - dess then for - get Par - a - phon - a - lia, Par - a - phon - a - lia? Can she the crown on an - oth - er head set Than of her Par - a - phon - a - lia? If that__ had__ not done__ too, Re- mem - ber__ my bone__ too, My bone, my bone, my bone. Sure my__ God - dess nev - er can For - get__ my mar - row - bone.

AIR XXI   Fair Dorinda   *Giovanni Battista Buononcini*

Oh Mis-ter Con-sta-ble,

Drunk-en   ras - cal, Would I had thee at_____ the Rose.

Mis - ter Con - sta-ble,   Drunk-en   ras - cal,   Mis-ter Con-sta - ble,

Drunk - en   ras - cal,   Would__ I   had thee   at__   the Rose.

Mayst thou be beat-en, Hanged up and eat - en,   Mayst thou be beat-en,

Hanged__ up and eat-en,   Eat - en by the__ car-_____ rion crows.

[Interlude]

The filth that lies__ in com - mon shores,__

May it ev - er Lie_____

D.C. al fine

in__ thy nose, Oh, may it lie__ in__ thy nose.

AIR XXII   Newmarket   *anon.*

Why, mad - am, do you give such words as these To a con - sta - ble and jus - tice of peace? I fan - cy you'll bet - ter know how to speak By that time you've been in Bride - well a week, Have beat - en good hemp— and been Whipped at a post; I hope you'll re - pent— when some skin You have lost. But if this— makes— you trem - ble, I'll not be sev-vere, Come down a good guin - ea and you shall be clear.

AIR XXIII   Charming Betty   *Henry Carey (?)*

Gen - tle preach-er, Non - con teach - er,

Pri - thee let us take__ a dance. Leave your cant - ing,

Zeal - ous rant - ing, Come and shake a

mer - ry haunch. Mo - tions fir - ing,

Sounds in - spir - ing, We are led__ to

sof - ter joys. Where in tran - ces,

Each soul dan-ces, Mus - ic then seems on - ly noise.

AIR XXIV   Gently Touch the Warbling Lyre   *Francesco Geminiani*

Let o - thers fond - ly court a throne,

All my joy's in you a - lone;

Let me find a crown in you,

Let me find a scep - ter too;

E- qual in the court or grove,

I am blest, do you but love.

AIR XXV   Oh Ponder Well   *anon.*

MONEYWOOD

A - lack how al - tered is my fate, What
chan - ges have I seen. For I, who lodg - ings
let of late, Am now a - gain a queen. And
I, who in this pup - pet show Have
played Punch - in - el - lo, Will now let all the
aud - ience know I am no com - mon fel - low.

Appendix D

Chronology

Approximate years are indicated by*.

Political and Literary Events	Life and Major Works of Fielding

1631
Shirley's *THE TRAITOR*.
Death of Donne.
John Dryden born.

1633
Samuel Pepys born.

1635
Sir George Etherege born.*

1640
Aphra Behn born.*

1641
William Wycherley born.*

1642
First Civil War began (ended 1646).
Theaters closed by Parliament.
Thomas Shadwell born.*

1648
Second Civil War.

1649
Execution of Charles I.

1650
Jeremy Collier born.

1651
Hobbes' *Leviathan* published.

1652
First Dutch War began (ended 1654).
Thomas Otway born.

1653
Nathaniel Lee born.*

1656
D'Avenant's *THE SIEGE OF RHODES* performed at Rutland House.

1657
John Dennis born.

1658
Death of Oliver Cromwell.
D'Avenant's *THE CRUELTY OF THE SPANIARDS IN PERU* performed at the Cockpit.

1660
Restoration of Charles II.
Theatrical patents granted to Thomas Killigrew and Sir William D'Avenant, authorizing them to form, respectively, the King's and the Duke of York's Companies.
Pepys began his diary.

1661
Cowley's *THE CUTTER OF COLEMAN STREET.*
D'Avenant's *THE SIEGE OF RHODES* (expanded to two parts.)

1662
Charter granted to the Royal Society.

1663
Dryden's *THE WILD GALLANT.*
Tuke's *THE ADVENTURES OF FIVE HOURS.*

1664
Sir John Vanbrugh born.
Dryden's *THE RIVAL LADIES.*
Dryden and Howard's *THE INDIAN QUEEN.*
Etherege's *THE COMICAL REVENGE.*

1665
Second Dutch War began (ended 1667).

Great Plague.
Dryden's *THE INDIAN EMPEROR*.
Orrery's *MUSTAPHA*.

1666
Fire of London.
Death of James Shirley.

1667
Milton's *Paradise Lost* published.
Sprat's *The History of the Royal Society* published.
Dryden's *SECRET LOVE*.

1668
Death of D'Avenant.
Dryden made Poet Laureate.
Dryden's *An Essay of Dramatic Poesy* published.
Shadwell's *THE SULLEN LOVERS*.

1669
Pepys terminated his diary.
Susannah Centlivre born.

1670
William Congreve born.
Dryden's *THE CONQUEST OF GRANADA*, Part I.

1671
Dorset Garden Theatre (Duke's Company) opened.
Colley Cibber born.
Milton's *Paradise Regained* and *Samson Agonistes* published.
Dryden's *THE CONQUEST OF GRANADA*, Part II.
THE REHEARSAL, by the Duke of Buckingham and others.
Wycherley's *LOVE IN A WOOD*.

1672
Third Dutch War began (ended 1674).
Joseph Addison born.
Richard Steele born.

Dryden's *MARRIAGE À LA MODE.*

1674

New Drury Lane Theatre (King's Company) opened.
Death of Milton.
Nicholas Rowe born.
Thomas Rymer's *Reflections on Aristotle's Treatise of Poesy* (translation of Rapin) published.

1675

Dryden's *AURENG-ZEBE.*
Wycherley's *THE COUNTRY WIFE.**

1676

Etherege's *THE MAN OF MODE.*
Otway's *DON CARLOS.*
Shadwell's *THE VIRTUOSO.*
Wycherley's *THE PLAIN DEALER.*

1677

Rymer's *Tragedies of the Last Age Considered* published.
Dryden's *ALL FOR LOVE.*
Lee's *THE RIVAL QUEENS.*
Behn's *THE ROVER.*

1678

Popish Plot.
George Farquhar born.
Bunyan's *Pilgrim's Progress* (Part I) published.

1679

Exclusion Bill introduced.
Death of Thomas Hobbes.
Death of Roger Boyle, Earl of Orrery.
Charles Johnson born.

1680

Death of Samuel Butler.
Death of John Wilmot, Earl of Rochester.
Dryden's *THE SPANISH FRIAR.*

Lee's *LUCIUS JUNIUS BRUTUS*.
Otway's *THE ORPHAN*.

1681

Charles II dissolved Parliament at Oxford.
Dryden's *Absalom and Achitophel* published.
Tate's adaptation of *KING LEAR*.

1682

The King's and the Duke of York's Companies merged into the United Company.
Dryden's *The Medal*, *MacFlecknoe*, and *Religio Laici* published.
Otway's *VENICE PRESERVED*.

1683

Rye House Plot.
Death of Thomas Killigrew.

1685

Death of Charles II; accession of James II.
Revocation of the Edict of Nantes.
The Duke of Monmouth's Rebellion.
Death of Otway.
John Gay born.
Crowne's *SIR COURTLY NICE*.
Dryden's *ALBION AND ALBANIUS*.

1687

Death of the Duke of Buckingham.
Dryden's *The Hind and the Panther* published.
Newton's *Principia* published.

1688

The Revolution.
Alexander Pope born.
Shadwell's *THE SQUIRE OF ALSATIA*.

1689

The War of the League of Augsburg began (ended 1697).

Toleration Act.

Death of Aphra Behn.

Shadwell made Poet Laureate.

Dryden's *DON SEBASTIAN.*

Shadwell's *BURY FAIR.*

1690

Battle of the Boyne.

Locke's *Two Treatises of Government* and *An Essay Concerning Human Understanding* published.

1691

Death of Etherege.

Langbaine's *An Account of the English Dramatic Poets* published.

1692

Death of Lee.

Death of Shadwell.

Tate made Poet Laureate.

1693

George Lillo born.*

Rymer's *A Short View of Tragedy* published.

Congreve's *THE OLD BACHELOR.*

1694

Death of Queen Mary.

Southerne's *THE FATAL MAR-RIAGE.*

1695

Group of actors led by Thomas Betterton leave Drury Lane and establish a new company at Lincoln's Inn Fields.

Congreve's *LOVE FOR LOVE.*

Southerne's *OROONOKO.*

1696

Cibber's *LOVE'S LAST SHIFT.*

Vanbrugh's *THE RELAPSE.*

1697

Treaty of Ryswick ended the War of the League of Augsburg.

Charles Macklin born.

Congreve's *THE MOURNING BRIDE.*

Vanbrugh's *THE PROVOKED WIFE*.

1698

Collier controversy started with the publication of *A Short View of the Immorality and Profaneness of the English Stage*.

1699

Farquhar's *THE CONSTANT COUPLE*.

1700

Death of Dryden.

Blackmore's *Satire against Wit* published.

Congreve's *THE WAY OF THE WORLD*.

1701

Act of Settlement.

War of the Spanish Succession began (ended 1713).

Death of James II.

Rowe's *TAMERLANE*.

Steele's *THE FUNERAL*.

1702

Death of William III; accession of Anne.

The Daily Courant began publication.

Cibber's *SHE WOULD AND SHE WOULD NOT*.

1703

Death of Samuel Pepys.

Rowe's *THE FAIR PENITENT*.

1704

Capture of Gibraltar; Battle of Blenheim.

Defoe's *The Review* began publication (1704–1713).

Swift's *A Tale of a Tub* and *The Battle of the Books* published.

Cibber's *THE CARELESS HUSBAND*.

1705

Haymarket Theatre opened.

Steele's *THE TENDER HUS-BAND*.

1706
Battle of Ramillies.
Farquhar's *THE RECRUITING OFFICER*.

1707
Union of Scotland and England.   Born April 22.
Death of Farquhar.
Farquhar's *THE BEAUX' STRATAGEM*.

1708
Downes' *Roscius Anglicanus* pub-lished.

1709
Samuel Johnson born.
Rowe's edition of Shakespeare pub-lished.
The Tatler began publication (1709–1710).
Centlivre's *THE BUSY BODY*.

1711
Shaftesbury's *Characteristics* pub-lished.
The Spectator began publication (1711–1712).
Pope's *An Essay on Criticism* pub-lished.

1713
Treaty of Utrecht ended the War of the Spanish Succession.
Addison's *CATO*.

1714
Death of Anne; accession of George I.
Steele became Governor of Drury Lane.
John Rich assumed management of Lincoln's Inn Fields.
Centlivre's *THE WONDER: A WOMAN KEEPS A SECRET*.
Rowe's *JANE SHORE*.

1715
Jacobite Rebellion.
Death of Tate.
Rowe made Poet Laureate.
Death of Wycherley.
1716
Addison's *THE DRUMMER.*
1717
David Garrick born.
Cibber's *THE NON-JUROR.*
Gay, Pope, and Arbuthnot's
*THREE HOURS AFTER
MARRIAGE.*
1718
Death of Rowe.
Centlivre's *A BOLD STROKE FOR
A WIFE.*
1719
Death of Addison.
Defoe's *Robinson Crusoe* published.
Young's *BUSIRIS, KING OF
EGYPT.*
1720
South Sea Bubble.
Samuel Foote born.
Little Theatre in the Haymarket
opened.
Steele suspended from the
Governorship of Drury Lane (re-
stored 1721).
Steele's *The Theatre* published.
Hughes' *THE SIEGE OF DAMAS-
CUS.*
1721
Walpole became first Minister.
1722
Steele's *THE CONSCIOUS
LOVERS.*
1723
Death of Susannah Centlivre.
Death of Durfey.
1725
Pope's edition of Shakespeare pub-
lished.

Entered Eton; remained there until
1725.*

1726
Death of Jeremy Collier.
Death of Vanbrugh.
Law's *Unlawfulness of Stage Entertainments* published.
Swift's *Gulliver's Travels* published.

1727
Death of George I; accession of George II.
Death of Sir Isaac Newton.
Arthur Murphy born.

1728
Pope's *The Dunciad* (First Version) published.
Cibber's *THE PROVOKED HUSBAND* (expansion of Vanbrugh's fragment *A JOURNEY TO LONDON*).
Gay's *THE BEGGAR'S OPERA*.

The Masquerade.
LOVE IN SEVERAL MASQUES (Drury Lane, February 16).
Enrolled at the University of Leyden.

1729
Goodman's Fields Theatre opened.
Death of Congreve.
Death of Steele.
Edmund Burke born.

Returned from Leyden.

1730
Cibber made Poet Laureate.
Oliver Goldsmith born.
Thomson's *The Seasons* published.

THE TEMPLE BEAU (Goodman's Fields, January 26).
THE AUTHOR'S FARCE (Haymarket, March 30).
TOM THUMB (Haymarket, April 24).
RAPE UPON RAPE (Haymarket, June 23).

1731
Death of Defoe.
Lillo's *THE LONDON MERCHANT*.

THE LETTER WRITERS (Haymarket, March 24).
THE TRAGEDY OF TRAGEDIES [revision of *TOM THUMB*] (Haymarket, March 24).
THE WELSH OPERA (Haymarket, April 22), revised as *THE GRUB STREET OPERA* (suppressed).

1732

Covent Garden Theatre opened.
Death of Gay.
George Colman the elder born.
Charles Johnson's *CAELIA*.

THE LOTTERY (Drury Lane, January 1).
THE MODERN HUSBAND (Drury Lane, February 14).
THE OLD DEBAUCHEES (Drury Lane, June 1).
THE COVENT GARDEN TRAGEDY (Drury Lane, June 1).
THE MOCK DOCTOR (Drury Lane, June 23).

1733

Pope's *An Essay on Man* (Epistles I–III) published (Epistle IV, 1734).

THE MISER (Drury Lane, February 17).

1734

Death of Dennis.
The Prompter began publication (1734–1736).
Theobald's edition of Shakespeare published.

THE AUTHOR'S FARCE, revised (Drury Lane, January 15).
THE INTRIGUING CHAMBERMAID (Drury Lane, January 15).
DON QUIXOTE IN ENGLAND (Haymarket, April 5).
Married Charlotte Cradock, November 28.

1735

Pope's *Epistle to Dr. Arbuthnot* published.

AN OLD MAN TAUGHT WISDOM (Drury Lane, January 6).
THE UNIVERSAL GALLANT (Drury Lane, February 10).

1736

Lillo's *FATAL CURIOSITY*.

Organized "Great Mogul's Company of Comedians" at the Haymarket.
PASQUIN (Haymarket, March 5).
TUMBLE-DOWN DICK (Haymarket, April 29).

1737

The Stage Licensing Act.
Dodsley's *THE KING AND THE MILLER OF MANSFIELD*.

EURYDICE (Drury Lane, February 19).
THE HISTORICAL REGISTER (Haymarket, March 21).
EURYDICE HISSED (Haymarket, April 13).
Entered the Middle Temple, November 1.

1738
Johnson's *London* published.
Pope's *One Thousand Seven Hundred and Thirty-Eight* published.
Swift's *A Complete Collection of Genteel and Ingenious Conversation* published.
Thomson's *AGAMENNON*.

1739
War with Spain began.
Death of Lillo.
Hugh Kelly born.
Johnson's *Complete Vindication of Licensers of the Stage*, an ironical criticism of the Licensing Act, published after Brooke's *GUSTAVUS VASA* was denied a license.

The Champion began publication (1739–1741).

1740
War of the Austrian Succession began (ended 1748).
James Boswell born.
Cibber's *Apology for His Life* published.
Richardson's *Pamela* published.
Garrick's *LETHE*.
Thomson and Mallet's *ALFRED*.

Called to the bar, June 20.

1741
Edmund Malone born.
Garrick began acting.
Dodsley's *THE BLIND BEGGAR OF BETHNAL GREEN*.
Garrick's *THE LYING VALET*.

Shamela published.

1742
Walpole resigned his offices.
Cibber's *Letters to Mr. Pope* published.
Collins's *Persian Eclogues* published.
Pope's *New Dunciad* (Book IV of *The Dunciad*) published.
Young's *The Complaint, or Night Thoughts* published (additional parts published each year until 1745).

Joseph Andrews published.
MISS LUCY IN TOWN (Drury Lane, May 6).

1743
Death of Henry Carey.

Miscellanies published.

Blair's *The Grave* published.

Hanmer's edition of Shakespeare published.

Pope's *The Dunciad* (final version) published.

THE WEDDING DAY (Drury Lane, February 17).

Death of his wife.*

1744

Death of Pope.

Death of Theobald.

Dodsley's *A Select Collection of Old Plays* published.

Johnson's *Life of Mr. Richard Savage* published.

Joseph Warton's *The Enthusiast* published.

1745

Jacobite Rebellion.

Death of Swift.

Thomas Holcroft born.

Johnson's *Observations on Macbeth* published.

Thomson's *TANCRED AND SIGIS-MUNDA*.

1746

Death of Southerne.

Collins's *Odes* published.

Joseph Warton's *Odes* published.

1747

Garrick entered the management of Drury Lane Theatre.

Johnson's *Prologue Spoken by Mr. Garrick at the Opening of the Theatre in Drury Lane, 1747.*

Warburton's edition of Shakespeare published.

Thomas Warton's *The Pleasures of Melancholy* published.

Garrick's *MISS IN HER TEENS*.

Hoadly's *THE SUSPICIOUS HUSBAND*.

Married Mary Daniel, November 27.

1748

Treaty of Aix-la-Chapelle ended the War of the Austrian Succession.

Death of Thomson.

Appointed Justice of Peace for Westminster.

Hume's *Philosophical Essays Concerning Human Understanding* published.
Richardson's *Clarissa* published.
Smollett's *Roderick Random* published.
Thomson's *The Castle of Indolence* published.

1749
Death of Ambrose Philips.   *Tom Jones* published.
Bolingbroke's *Idea of a Patriot King* published.
Chetwood's *A General History of the Stage* published.
Johnson's *The Vanity of Human Wishes* published.
Hill's *MEROPE* (adaptation of Voltaire).
Johnson's *IRENE*.

1750
Death of Aaron Hill.
Johnson's *The Rambler* began publication (1750–1752).

1751
Death of Bolingbroke.
Richard Brinsley Sheridan born.
Gray's *An Elegy Wrote in a Country Churchyard* published.
Smollett's *Peregrine Pickle* published.

1752
Mason's *ELFRIDA* published.   *Amelia* published.
                                                   The Covent Garden Journal published.

1753
Death of Bishop Berkeley.
Elizabeth Inchbald born.
Foote's *THE ENGLISHMAN IN PARIS*.
Glover's *BOADICEA*.
Moore's *THE GAMESTER*.
Young's *THE BROTHERS*.

1754
Richardson's *Sir Charles Grandison*   Died in Lisbon, October 8.
published.

Whitehead's *CREUSA, QUEEN OF ATHENS.*

1755

Johnson's *A Dictionary of the English Language* published.

John Brown's *BARBAROSSA.*

Journal of a Voyage to Lisbon published.

1756

Seven Years War began.

William Godwin born.

Burke's *A Philosophical Enquiry into . . . the Sublime and Beautiful* published.

First part of Joseph Warton's *Essay on . . . Pope* published (second part, 1782).

Murphy's *THE APPRENTICE.*

1757

Battle of Plassey (India).

Death of Cibber.

Death of Moore.

William Blake born.

Gray's *Odes* published.

Home's *DOUGLAS* (performed the year before in Edinburgh).